ESTRENO Collection of Contemporary Spanish Plays

General Editor: Martha T. Halsey

THE SLEEP OF REASON

ANTONIO BUERO-VALLEJO

THE SLEEP OF REASON
(El sueño de la razón)

Translated by Marion Peter Holt

ESTRENO
University Park, Pennsylvania
1998

ESTRENO Contemporary Spanish Plays 14
General Editor: Martha T. Halsey
                  Department of Spanish, Italian and Portuguese
                  College of the Liberal Arts
                  The Pennsylvania State University
                  University Park, PA 16802 USA

Library of Congress Cataloging-in-Publication Data
Buero-Vallejo, Antonio, 1916-
        The Sleep of Reason
        Translation of: El sueño de la razón
        Contents: The Sleep of Reason
        1. Buero-Vallejo, Antonio, 1916-   Translation, English
I. Holt, Marion Peter. II. Title
Library of Congress Catalog Card No.: 98-70409
ISBN: 1-888463-04-X

This play was translated under a grant from
The National Endowment for the Arts

Published with support from
Program for Cultural Cooperation
Spanish Ministry of Education and Culture and United States' Universities

Cover: Jeffrey Eads

A NOTE ON THE PLAY

In *The Sleep of Reason* by Antonio Buero-Vallejo, we encounter the aging Spanish painter Francisco de Goya. The year is 1823, and at the age of seventy-six Goya is now completely deaf. In addition to suffering the burden of his physical handicap, he is beset by an array of daunting problems: not only is his life in danger because of his opposition to the absolutist power of the king, but he suspects his friends and loved ones of betrayal; and in addition to his crumbling family and home life, he must contend with his disintegrating mental condition. Goya's anguish over these circumstances is reflected in the famous, almost nightmarish "Black Paintings" which cover the walls of his country home. The play's title, taken from a well-known etching by Goya, poetically conveys the truth of his predicament: his sense of reason has fallen asleep, and in order to survive the difficulties he now faces, he must try to awaken it and take control of his life.

Buero-Vallejo expertly bridges the gulf that so often exists between the stage and an audience by means of his trademark "immersion effects" which some critics have linked to the theories of both Artaud and Brecht. Through the use of these ingenious techniques, the playwright draws the audience into the play by allowing it to enter the sensorial world of a main character. In *The Sleep of Reason*, Buero-Vallejo forces us to participate in Goya's exhausting frustration by experiencing his deafness. Whenever the old man enters the stage, our own world suddenly falls silent: like Goya, we can't hear the other characters speak, we can't hear their footsteps, the sounds they make—nothing but total silence, and the beating of our own hearts. And as we share in Goya's despairing sense of isolation, confusion, and vulnerability, we wonder if we have invaded the spectacle, or if the spectacle has invaded us.

This uniquely theatrical relationship between the audience and the stage in *The Sleep of Reason* is intensified by Buero-Vallejo's masterful use of multimedia effects. Through a rich and multivalent composition of sound cues, lighting changes, and slide projections, we witness the intrusion of Goya's fantastic imagination and inner thoughts on his surface reality. On several occasions we hear the disembodied voice of his daughter Mariquita speaking to him; throughout the play we see the "Black Paintings" appear and fade across the set, either reflecting his state-of-mind or commenting on a situation; and in certain scenes, we hear a loud, throbbing heartbeat invade Goya's and even other characters' minds. This juxtaposition of Goya's inner world with his outer world provides a powerful insight into his disintegrating mental and spiritual condition. The play is subtitled "a fantasia in two parts," and like the complex musical counterpoint of a Bach *fantasie*, Buero-Vallejo arranges the scenic elements into

vii

a sometimes brutal, sometimes beautiful symphony of subjective and objective harmonies.

   Although Antonio Buero-Vallejo won international acclaim for this play after its first production in Madrid in 1970, he has yet to be as fully embraced by the American theater community as some of his northern European counterparts. In this sterling translation by Marion Peter Holt, however, *The Sleep of Reason* reveals itself to be a breathtaking and highly original theatrical achievement, as innovative in form as it is provocative in content. And while its technical requirements may prove challenging to many theaters, the play's distinctive and profound contribution to the art of theater earns it a place on stages throughout America.

Christopher de Haan
Yale University

ABOUT THE PLAYWRIGHT

Antonio Buero-Vallejo is Spain's preeminent post-Lorcan dramatist. Since his early recognition in 1949 as recipient of the prestigious Lope de Vega Prize for Drama, he has written more than two dozen plays. Some of his finest dramas, such as *Las Meninas* (1960), *The Sleep of Reason* (1970), and *The Foundation* (1974), contain encoded statements against censorship, authoritarianism, and internecine wars peculiar to Spain's own troubled political history, yet they easily transcend the time and place of their initial productions and remain major theatrical works of enduring relevance. In *Secret Dialogue* (1984) and *The Music Window* (1989), he addresses the social problems of post-Franco Spain, but these plays also focus on individual struggles to which audiences in any country can relate.

With only a few exceptions, Buero's plays contain scenic elements that are inextricably linked to their dramatic unfolding, as co-signifiers or iconic references. In his most complex scenic concepts, lighting and sound are both specific and interrelated to create a total dramatic experience in which aesthetic distance is diminished or even momentarily eliminated. The devices most typical of the Buerian mode are abrupt visual or aural transformations which draw the spectator into the actual physical experience of the character on stage. These have included absolute darkness (for blindness), absolute silence (for deafness), the draining of color from the set (for colorblindness), and onstage depictions of the illusion or delusion of a character that are shared by the audience. The expression "immersion-effects" has become standard to describe these devices—although Buero himself has also used the equally descriptive term "interiorization" on occasion. The pure or total immersion-effects invariably involve a physical experience on the part of the spectator if the effect is properly achieved in a technical sense. Other effects tend to stimulate the audience psychologically rather than physically. They are generally ancillary to the moment, trigger a thematic, metafictional, or identity association that intensifies the dramatic experience, preventing the spectator from merely viewing an action performed within a frame. In many instances this type of Buerian immersion is initiated by a musical phrase or motif that may contain multiple suggestions.

The Sleep of Reason is Buero's most widely performed play. After its original production in Madrid in 1970, the play was staged in Rostock, Moscow, Budapest, Oslo, Tokyo, and in Warsaw by the acclaimed director Andrzej Wajda. The English version had its professional premiere at Baltimore's Center Stage in 1984 and has also been staged in Philadelphia (1986), London (1991) and Chicago (1994).

ix

Antonio Buero-Vallejo.

CHARACTERS
(In order of appearance)

FRANCISCO TADEO CALOMARDE
KING FERDINAND VII
FRANCISCO DE GOYA
LEOCADIA ZORRILLA WEISS
EUGENIO ARRIETA
GUMERSINDA GOICOECHEA
JOSÉ DUASO Y LATRE
THE BAT FIGURE
THE HORNED FIGURE
FIRST CARNIVAL FIGURE
SECOND CARNIVAL FIGURE
THE CAT FIGURE
SERGEANT OF THE ROYAL VOLUNTEERS
FIRST VOLUNTEER
SECOND VOLUNTEER
THIRD VOLUNTEER
FOURTH VOLUNTEER
VOICE OF MARIA WEISS (MARIQUITA)
OTHER VOICES

The action takes place in Madrid, December 1823

Note: All the dialogue enclosed in guillemets (« ») is mouthed by the characters silently, and it only serves the purpose of orienting the actors. The director may, therefore, elaborate on these unheard auxiliary speeches. All of the passages of dialogue in quotation marks are actual Goya texts. It is possible for the actors who perform the figures in the dream sequence to double as the Royal Volunteers. Other doubling may be feasible.

PART ONE
Scene 1

The setting vaguely suggests the two rooms, downstairs and upstairs, of the house GOYA decorated with his "Black Paintings."* The diagonal doorway at stage left reveals the first steps of an inner stairway; the entrance at right, another room. Near the upstage wall there is a ladder which the painter uses for working on the walls and a chest on top of which are a shotgun, a palette, and a conglomeration of paint pots, brushes, and bottles of oil and varnish. There is a small painting turned against the wall. Downstage right, a work table with engravings, paper, albums, pencils, a small silver bell, and a table clock. Behind it, an armchair. At left, a smaller chair. Downstage left, a round platform with a cup-shaped brazier, surrounded by chairs and a sofa. A scattering of chairs or stools in the corners.

Total darkness. The lights come up slowly on a small area downstage to reveal a man seated in a regal chair He is absorbed in a curious task: embroidering neatly and carefully on a frame. As the lighted area widens, we see another man standing at his right; and at his left, a small table with a sewing basket, a spyglass, and a pistol. The seated man is KING FERDINAND VII. He looks about forty and is dressed in dark colors. A decoration sparkles on his breast. His overall appearance is vigorous; his calves are notably robust. Dark sideburns frame his fleshy cheeks; a fringe of hair half-covers his forehead. Under the thick brows, two very dark and inquisitive pupils. His nose, thick and flattened, rides over two thin lips which are submerged by the advance of the chin and which are usually smiling. The man who accompanies him is DON FRANCISCO TADEO CALOMARDE. He appears to be fifty and is also dressed in dark colors. His hair tousled over a smooth forehead; two shining little eyes gleam in his sheep-like features.

CALOMARDE: Your Majesty embroiders beautifully.

KING: You flatter me, Calomarde.

CALOMARDE: Credit where credit is due, sir. Such shadings! Such a sense of detail!

KING: I had a lot of practice in Valençay, to calm my nerves when I was in exile. (*Brief pause*) It wouldn't be a bad thing if all Spaniards learned to embroider. Maybe they'd be more docile.

CALOMARDE: (*Very serious*) It would be a good Christian discipline. Does Your Majesty wish me to draw up the decree?

KING: (*Laughing*) You're not a minister yet, Tadeo. (*Stitching*) What are they saying in Madrid?

---

*A list of Goya's "Black Paintings" is provided at the end of the text of the play.

CALOMARDE: There's high praise for Your Majesty. The summary executions and the banishments have left the liberal Hydra without a head. The patriots think it's as good as dead . . . provided a firm hand is applied.

KING: There will be a firm hand. But without the Inquisition. I don't want to restore it now.

CALOMARDE: The country is asking for it, sir.

KING: The priests are asking for it, you mean. If I'm to have absolute power, I don't want a meddling Inquisition.

CALOMARDE: (*Sighing*) May God grant that 1824 be like an implacable hammer for subversives and Masons of every stripe.*

KING: (*Raising his hand and interrupting him coldly*) What else are they talking about?

CALOMARDE: (*Softly*) About the Green Book, sir. (*The KING gives him a look.*) Even though no one has ever seen it.

KING: I can assure you it does exist . . .

CALOMARDE: Then, sir, why keep it hidden?

KING: It's an account of wrongs committed against my person.

CALOMARDE: Which therefore deserve prompt punishment.

KING: (*Smiles*) Time is needed to weave a rope.

CALOMARDE: Your majesty prefers to gather evidence.

KING: Something like that.

CALOMARDE: (*Handing him a damaged piece of paper after a moment*) Such as this?

KING: (*Taking the piece of paper*) What is it?

CALOMARDE: An intercepted letter, sir. (*The KING reads it, and his expression changes. Then he reflects.*)

KING: Did you witness the execution of Riego?

CALOMARDE: A month ago, sir.

KING: (*Leaving the letter on the table*) Many accounts of it have reached me. . . . What is your version?

CALOMARDE: It was a solemn day. All Madrid was shouting your name when a donkey dragged the condemned man by in a basket.

KING: One might say an etching by Goya.

CALOMARDE: (*Looking at him, curious*) Precisely, sir . . . Riego mounted the scaffold weeping and kissing the steps, begging for pardon like a frightened whore. . .

KING: You saw all this?

CALOMARDE: Everyone in Madrid saw it.

KING: Then he was afraid.

---

*Several different Masonic orders were established in Spain in the early 1800s. The Masons (or Freemasons) were anathema to Fernando VII because of their liberal aims.

CALOMARDE: He'd already recanted in writing.

KING: Under torture?

CALOMARDE: (*Looking away*) If he'd been tortured, he was no longer suffering, but he was afraid. The "hero" of Las Cabezas,* the charlatan of the Cortes,† that small-time general, was smelling of fear. As they dragged him by, the crowds were laughing and holding their noses.

KING: (*With a grimace of revulsion*) Spare me the details.

CALOMARDE: Why not say, sir, that the liberal vainglory ended with an attack of diarrhea?

KING: Because they're not all so cowardly.

CALOMARDE: Is Your Majesty perhaps thinking of the author of that letter?

KING: Anyone who writes that way today is either a fool or a brave man.

CALOMARDE: A witless dummy, sir, like all that cowardly band of poets and painters! Look how many of them have escaped to France.

KING: Not he.

CALOMARDE: He's hidden himself in his country place on the other side of the river. Like a child who closes his eyes and imagines he's safe, he thinks Your Majesty can't reach him. Nevertheless, from this very balcony you can see his house with your spyglass. (*He hands it to him. The KING puts his embroidery aside, stands, adjusts the spyglass and points it toward the audience.*)

KING: Is it that house near the Segovia Bridge?

CALOMARDE: The second one, at left.

KING: I can hardly see it for the trees. . . . He hasn't come to pay me homage since I returned to Madrid.

CALOMARDE: Or to collect his wages, sir. He doesn't dare.

KING: What do you suppose he's doing?

CALOMARDE: Trembling.

KING: That peasant doesn't tremble so easily. He was always a proud and stubborn man. When I asked him to paint the face of my first wife in his portrait of the royal family, he told me he didn't retouch his canvases.

CALOMARDE: Outrageous!

KING: Only an excuse of his. The real reason was that he detested me. Of course, I paid him back in the same coin. He's painted me only a few times, and my wives not at all.

CALOMARDE: A light punishment, sir. That letter . . .

*Las Cabezas: Cabezas de San Juan, the town where Colonel Rafael de Riego Nuñez initiated a liberal uprising in 1820. Riego, a hero in the struggle against the French invaders, was publicly humiliated and then executed for treason on November 7, 1823.

†Las Cortes: the Cortes (or Parliament) of Cadiz which proclaimed the Spanish constitution of 1812, curtailing the power of the king.

Rick Stoppleworth and Robert McCallum in *The Sleep of Reason*.
Philadelphia, 1986. Directed by Blanka Zizka.
Photo: The Wilma Theatre.

KING: We must think it over.

CALOMARDE: He's not the great painter they say, sir! Artless drawings, harsh colors . . . *(The KING lowers his spyglass.)* Royal portraits without dignity or beauty . . . Insidious engravings against the dynasty, against the clergy . . . Now Vicente López is a great painter.

KING: Such severity, Tadeo! Has he offended you in some way?

CALOMARDE: Much less than he has offended Your Majesty. He did refuse to paint my portrait once. *(The KING glances at him.)* But my feelings have nothing to do with trivialities. . . . It is the enemy of King and country that I hate.

KING: *(Smiling)* What do you recommend for our hotheaded painter? The same death as Riego's?

CALOMARDE: *(Softly)* It was Your Majesty who thought of that when he read the letter.

KING: *(Resuming his embroidering)* His prestige is great.

CALOMARDE: He deserves the gallows for that piece of paper. *(A moment of silence. He leans over again to appreciate the KING'S embroidery.)* What exquisite greens, sir! Embroidery is a form of painting. . . . *(Smiling)* Your Majesty paints better than that senile old fool.

KING: *(After a moment)* To whom was it addressed?

CALOMARDE: Martín Zapater, sir. A friend of his from childhood.

KING: Is he a Mason? A Comunero?*

CALOMARDE: There's no information on him . . . I'm investigating.

(A dull heartbeat becomes audible. The KING looks up quickly from his work. The beating increases in intensity and speeds up until it culminates in three or four heavy thuds, followed by others which are softer and spaced out. The KING stands up before the sound stops and steps back toward the left. A silence)

KING: What was that sound?

CALOMARDE: *(Perplexed)* I don't know, sir.

KING: Go see.

(CALOMARDE exits right. The KING takes the pistol from the table and clutches it. CALOMARDE returns.)

---

*Comunero: a member of the "Confederación de Caballeros Comuneros," a liberal secret society similar to Masonry that flourished in Spain during the brief period of constitutional government (1820-23) prior to the autocratic rule of Fernando VII. Like the Masons, they were considered traitors by the king.

CALOMARDE: They didn't hear anything outside, sir.

KING: There was a noise, wasn't there?

CALOMARDE: (*Stammering*) A faint noise.

KING: Faint? (*He puts the pistol down, sits, and returns to his embroidery pensively.*) Have the guard doubled tonight.

CALOMARDE: Yes, Majesty.

KING: (*He embroiders; then stops.*) I don't want fighting cocks. I want obedient vassals, who tremble. And an ocean of tears for all the insults to my person.

CALOMARDE: (*Quietly*) Very just, sir. (*The KING embroiders.*)

KING: Listen, Calomarde. This is confidential. You will tell the Commander General of the Royal Volunteers to come to see me tomorrow at ten.

CALOMARDE: (*Quietly*) It will be done, sir.

KING: (*After a moment*) And Don José Duaso . . . (*He breaks off.*)

CALOMARDE: . . . Father Duaso.

KING: You will say that I expect him, too.

CALOMARDE: At the same hour?

KING: Later. Don't let them see each other. At three in the afternoon.

CALOMARDE: I understand.

KING: Isn't Father Duaso Aragonese?

CALOMARDE: Aragonese, sir, like me. (*Brief pause*) And like Don Francisco de Goya. (*They exchange glances. The KING smiles and applies himself to his embroidery. Slow fade.*)

Scene 2

When the lights come up again, we see downstage an old man who is looking through a spyglass toward the audience. Goya's "Aquelarre" ("Witches' Sabbath") is projected gradually on the background. The hair and sideburns of the short but vigorous and erect old man are now white. He is wearing an old smock covered with paint splotches. When he lowers the spyglass, he reveals surly and unmistakable facial features: those of FRANCISCO DE GOYA. The aged painter looks through the spyglass again. He sighs, goes to the table, leaves the instrument there and picks up a pair of eyeglasses which he puts on. He turns around and looks at the projected painting for a few seconds. Then he goes over to the chest, takes palette and brushes, climbs on the ladder and gives a few brushstrokes to the "Aquelarre." Suddenly we hear a soft meowing. GOYA stops without turning his head and presently continues painting. Another meow. He stops again. The meows are repeated; they come from several cats almost simultaneously. GOYA shakes his head and covers an ear with his free hand. Silence. He gets down from the ladder puts aside his equipment, and walks around the stage looking into the corners. A long meow forces him to look toward the doorway. Silence. The painter tosses his glasses on the table, takes off his smock, and screams out in his shrill deaf-man's voice.

GOYA: Leo! (*Brief pause*) Leocadia! (*He goes to the sofa and picks up a large frock coat.*) Isn't there anyone at home? (*Putting on the coat, he goes to the door.*) Child! Mariquita!

(He waits anxiously. We hear the laughter of an eight-year-old child. A feeble, far-off strange laughter which is suddenly cut off. Upset, GOYA returns to center stage and puts his hands over his ears. In an outburst of silent fury, he seizes the little bell from the table and shakes it repeatedly, without making the slightest sound. DOÑA LEOCADIA ZORRILLA enters left, with angry gestures and hurling inaudible words. She is a woman of thirty-five, not unattractive but far from being beautiful; a haughty Basque with dark hair, firm limbs, and vivid eyes under her dark brows.)

LEOCADIA: «What's all the shouting about? What's your hurry? Did a scorpion bite you?»

GOYA: (*Sourly*) What are you saying? (*LEOCADIA sighs—which we don't hear either—and rapidly forms letters in Bonet's alphabet* with her right hand.*) No, I haven't been stung by a scorpion! Where's the child?

LEOCADIA: (*Pointing right*) «In there.»

GOYA: You lie! I've called her and she doesn't come. Where have you sent her?

LEOCADIA: (*Not at all bothered by her lie*) «For a walk.»

GOYA: (*Angrily*) With your hand! (*LEOCADIA forms signs and shouts inaudibly in anger at the same time.*)

LEOCADIA: «For a walk!»

GOYA: For a walk in these times? (*He takes her by the wrist.*) Are you out of your mind?

LEOCADIA: (*Struggling*) «Let go!»

GOYA: You don't act like her mother! But you are, and you're supposed to look after your children! Your days of partying and flaunting yourself are over.

LEOCADIA: (*Speaking incessantly at the same time*) «Of course I am! And I know what to do. And I'll send them where I please! Besides, who are you to be giving me lessons! . . . »

---

*The system of sign language used in Spain in Goya's time. It was invented by Juan Pablo Bonet (1560-1620?), a Spanish writer and diplomat who dedicated a great part of his life to improving the condition of the deaf.

GOYA: (*Her gesticulating makes him furious. Shouting*) I'm fed up with your angry looks! (*LEOCADIA steps back disdainfully and makes a few signs.*) Well and fine! But she shouldn't be in the orchard either if there's no one with her. (*LEOCADIA signs.*) Her brother's a child too! (*He strides brusquely to the left.*) Where have you put my hat and cane? (*She points right. When GOYA starts to leave, we hear a meow. He stops, turns around and looks at LEOCADIA. She questions him with a movement of her head.*)

LEOCADIA: «Where are you going?»

GOYA: I can't paint today! (*He starts to leave and turns around again.*) Where are the cats now?

LEOCADIA: (*Puzzled, she uses sign language.*) «In the kitchen.»

GOYA: Did you see them in the kitchen? (*She nods.*) Of course. Where else would they be? Goodbye.

(*He exits. LEOCADIA hurries to the door and watches him go. Then she makes a signal, and DOCTOR ARRIETA, hat and cane in hand, enters cautiously. DON EUGENIO GARCIA ARRIETA is between fifty-five and sixty. He is vigorous but gaunt. His blond hair is turning gray; he hides his incipient baldness by combing his hair forward; he has a large cranium and the sharp features of an ascetic; his eyes have a gentle and melancholy look. He is about to speak but LEOCADIA motions him to keep silent. A door slams in the distance.*)

ARRIETA: You shouldn't have let him go out.

LEOCADIA: I wanted to speak with you first. (*She goes to the sofa and sits.*) Please sit down, Doctor Arrieta.

ARRIETA: (*Taking a chair*) Thank you, señora. Maria de Rosario and little Guillermo, are they well?

LEOCADIA: Yes, thanks to God. They're not at home now. (*She stirs the brazier.*) We'll have snow for Christmas.

ARRIETA: What's wrong with Don Francisco? (*Goya's "Saturn" is projected to the right of the "Witches' Sabbath."*)

LEOCADIA: Doctor, you cured him four years ago. Cure him for me now.

ARRIETA: Of what?

LEOCADIA: It's nothing you can see. No pains, or cough, or fever. Only his deafness, but you already know about that. (*She wrings her hands nervously.*) And that's why I asked you to come. Three years ago you made the effort to learn sign language to speak with him. You must talk to him to cure him, and it will be difficult.

ARRIETA: Tell me everything you can, señora. (*Goya's "Judith" appears at the left of the "Witches' Sabbath."*)

LEOCADIA: For the past two years he's almost never gone away from the house; he almost never speaks.

ARRIETA: Withdrawn, unsociable . . . It's not an illness.

LEOCADIA: Have you noticed the paintings on the walls?

ARRIETA. (*He studies the projected paintings.*) These?

LEOCADIA: And all the ones upstairs. He was an artist who never retouched, but he retouches these endlessly. What do you think of them?

ARRIETA: They're strange.

LEOCADIA: They're appalling! (*She stands and walks about.*)

ARRIETA: I remember similar things in his etchings.

LEOCADIA: They weren't the same. These are the horrible paintings of an old man.

ARRIETA: Don Francisco is an old man.

LEOCADIA: (*She stops and looks at him.*) A demented old man.

ARRIETA. (*Getting up slowly*) Are you suggesting he's lost his mind? (*She closes her eyes and nods.*) What evidence do you have? Only the paintings?

LEOCADIA: (*Listening*) Be quiet! (*A moment of silence*) Did you hear something?

ARRIETA: No.

LEOCADIA: (*Taking a few steps left*) It must have been the cats in the kitchen. . . . (*Turning back to him*) He hardly ever talks with me, but he talks with someone. . . who doesn't exist. Or he laughs for no reason, or lashes out against invisible beings. Look at that. Doesn't it frighten you?

ARRIETA: (*Facing the "Witches' Sabbath"*) The devil, the witches . . . He doesn't believe in witches, señora. These paintings may be frightening to you, but they're the work of a satirist, not a madman.

LEOCADIA: Those paintings are about me.

(*ARRIETA stops before "Judith" and looks back at LEOCADIA.*)

ARRIETA: About you?

(*The "Witches' Sabbath" changes into "Asmodea" ["Fantastic Vision"].*)

LEOCADIA: (*Nodding*) He says I'm the witch who's drying up his blood. Look at that one! (*ARRIETA faces the "Asmodea."*) The woman is leading the man to the Witches' Sabbath, and he's terrified, with his mouth gagged with an evil stone. I'm the woman. (*As she speaks, "Saturn" changes to "The Busybodies." ARRIETA studies them.*) You would have to live with us to understand how . . . insane he's become.

ARRIETA: This scene . . . does it refer to you too? (*LEOCADIA turns around and is silent for a moment when she sees the painting.*)

LEOCADIA: I don't know. (*ARRIETA looks at the painting and observes LEOCADIA.*)

ARRIETA: (*Puzzled*) What are they doing?

LEOCADIA: He hasn't said.

ARRIETA: But you have some idea. (*A silence*) Or don't you?

LEOCADIA: I think it's . . . an obscene painting.

ARRIETA: Obscene?

LEOCADIA: (*Embarrassed*) Don't you see it? Those two girls are making fun of . . . that poor old fool's pleasure.

(*Very surprised, ARRIETA looks at the painting again. Then he studies the "Asmodea" and "Judith." LEOCADIA is looking at the floor. ARRIETA goes to her side.*)

ARRIETA: How old is Goya now?

LEOCADIA: Seventy-six.

ARRIETA: (*Hesitating*) Permit me a very delicate question. (*She looks at him uneasily.*) When did you stop having intimate relations?

LEOCADIA: We've never stopped. Not completely at least.

ARRIETA: (*Sitting down beside her*) Not completely?

LEOCADIA: (*With difficulty*) Francho . . . Excuse me . . . We call him Francho at home. Don Francisco is one of those men who stays young until late in life. When he began to court me, I permitted his advances because I was curious . . . and amused. But when he actually made love to me, I was like a lamb in the jaws of a great wolf. He was sixty-four then.

ARRIETA: And now, twelve years later.

LEOCADIA: He still desires me . . . occasionally. Oh, my God! For months on end he avoids me at night and never speaks to me by day. . . because . . . he's no longer so vigorous. . . . (*ARRIETA takes a melancholy look at the paintings and appears to be in deep thought.*)

ARRIETA: (*Calmly*) Doña Leocadia . . . (*She is extremely uncomfortable when she looks at him.*) Do you have any reason to suspect that Don Francisco . . . attends to his needs like the old man in the painting?

LEOCADIA: (*Avoiding his eyes*) I don't know.

ARRIETA: How old are you now?

LEOCADIA: Thirty-five. (*A brief pause*) Shhh! Don't you hear something? (*She gets up and goes left to listen.*) It must be the servants.

ARRIETA: I'll examine him. But you need attention too. I find you nervous and distraught. Perhaps a change of scene would help.

LEOCADIA: (*Turning to him, forcefully*) He's the one who needs a change! Let's not talk about me any more, please. Francho's madness is just that! He refuses a change of scene! He's not afraid.

ARRIETA: I don't understand.

LEOCADIA: (*With growing agitation*) Do you know that no one comes to see us, Doctor?

ARRIETA: You live in an out-of-the-way place.

LEOCADIA: That's their excuse! The truth is they know he was on the losing side and that the king hates him.

ARRIETA: You must not say that, señora.

LEOCADIA: You know very well it's true. Every day people are banished, whipped, and executed. . . . Francho is one of the liberals, and in Spain there'll be no mercy for them for years to come. The hunt has begun, and they'll come for him too. And he knows it! (*Transition*) But he remains indifferent. He paints, he shouts at the servants, he goes for walks . . . And when I beg him to take precautions, to escape like so many of his friends, he insists there's no reason to. Isn't that madness?

ARRIETA: Perhaps he's exhausted.

LEOCADIA: Not as exhausted as I am! You have to be insane not to be afraid. I have all my wits about me, and I'm afraid. (*She moves close to ARRIETA.*) Give him the fear he needs, Doctor. Force him to leave!

ARRIETA: (*Standing up*) It can be fatal to make an old person afraid.

LEOCADIA: (*With a strange hope in her voice as she uses all her powers of persuasion.*) Then don't scare him. Tell him he needs a change . . . that the waters at a French resort would help him.

ARRIETA: I'll think it over, Doña Leocadia. (*She gives him a pleading look, sighs, and sits again. Suddenly she loses control and lets out a wracking sob. ARRIETA goes to her with compassion.*) Are you ill?

LEOCADIA: I can't stand it. (*A door slams offstage. She looks up.*) Now I do hear something.

GOYA'S VOICE: Didn't the postman come today?

LEOCADIA: It's Francho.

GOYA: You never know anything. (*The voice comes nearer.*) Go back to the kitchen!

LEOCADIA: (*Pleading*) Help us. (*They look left. GOYA enters and stops when he sees them. LEOCADIA stands up.*)

GOYA: Doctor Arrieta! (*LEOCADIA takes his hat and cane and puts them on a chair.*) We've missed you in this house! (*He embraces the DOCTOR effusively.*) As a friend, of course! We'd hate to need you as a physician. (*ARRIETA smiles. LEOCADIA helps GOYA take off his coat.*) Sit down! Leo, bring two glasses of wine. (*The DOCTOR shakes his head.*) Really! If you don't drink, I will! Or is it forbidden to me? (*ARRIETA makes a gesture of doubt.*) I assure you I'm as strong as a bull!

ARRIETA: (*Laughing*) «That's easy to see.» (*He sits.*)

GOYA: There's nothing like the open spaces for the good life, Don Eugenio. These hills are the essence of health itself. You'll see the color in Mariquita's cheeks. Has she come back, Leo? I looked for her when I went out but I didn't see her. (*LEOCADIA nods quickly.*) Have you seen her, Doctor? (*ARRIETA shakes his head.*) Well, bring her, woman! And the wine! (*With a questioning gesture, LEOCADIA speaks with her hands. GOYA'S voice loses its exuberance.*) I turned back at the bridge.

LEOCADIA: (*With a look of concern*) «Why?»

GOYA: They've installed a platoon of the Royal Volunteers, and they're stopping everyone.

LEOCADIA: (*Disturbed, she goes to his side.*) «There was none there before.»

GOYA: They must have assigned them today. (*She questions with her hands.*) How do I know how long they're going to stay! I can't stand their criminal faces and stupid laughter. I certainly wasn't going to tell them I'm deaf, even if I didn't understand what they were saying. So I came back. Bring the wine. The doctor is waiting. (*She nods and runs left.*) Wait! (*She stops.*) Has the postman come? (*She shakes her head and exits. GOYA sits and stirs the brazier with a poker. "The Busy bodies" changes into "Leocadia" and "Asmodea" into "The Holy Office."*) I'll bet she told you I'm sick and that we should run off to France. (*ARRIETA is momentarily speechless. He laughs.*) She dreams of France. It's boring here. (*Becoming aroused*) But why the devil should I go? This is my house, this is my country! I haven't gone back to the palace, and old flat nose doesn't like my paintings. For ten years he's had that mealymouthed, sanctimonious Vicente López do his portraits. It's better that way. I, in my house, unremembered, and painting what I feel like painting. But tell me what's happening in Madrid. (*ARRIETA opens his arms in a gesture of dismay.*) No, don't say anything. Accusations, persecutions . . . Spain. It's not easy to paint. But I shall. Have you noticed the walls? (*ARRIETA avoids an answer and asks a question in sign language.*) Afraid? No. (*He thinks about it.*) Sad, perhaps. (*The sound of light heartbeats. GOYA perceives them.*) No, not afraid. (*LEOCADIA reappears with a crockery pitcher and two glasses on a tray. ARRIETA gets up and accepts one of the glasses with a bow. "Judith" is transformed into the "Two Friars." GOYA takes the other glass.*) The wine will cure your troubles, doctor. To your health. (*They touch glasses and drink, LEOCADIA deposits the tray on the table. The heartbeats fade quickly when the painter drains his glass. LEOCADIA moves downstage and looks out toward the left from an imaginary balcony.*) Excellent, isn't it? Martin Zapater sent me a whole skin of it, so that I'd forgive him for not coming to spend a few days. He's so tied down in Zaragoza. (*He breaks off and resumes in a loud, harsh voice that catches LEOCADIA and the DOCTOR off guard.*) What are you looking at?

LEOCADIA: (*Turning around and responding weakly*) «The . . . bridge.»

GOYA: There's nothing you have to see on the bridge.

LEOCADIA: (*Surprised*) «Why not?»

GOYA: Bring your children so they can see the doctor! (*LEOCADIA mutters to herself and exits left with a gesture of dismay to ARRIETA behind the painter's back. The heartbeats have resumed, and GOYA nervously presses his ear with a finger. Then he leaves his glass on the tray and goes upstage.*) Come here, Don Eugenio. What do you think? (*ARRIETA follows him upstage, still holding his glass from which he sips while puckering his lips approvingly. They are standing before "The Holy Office."*) Don't they resemble animals? They're looking at us, not realizing how ugly they are. They're looking at me.

ARRIETA: «At you?»

GOYA: Exactly as they did when they denounced me to the Holy Inquisition. They looked at me like insects with their insect eyes because I'd painted a nude woman. They're insects that believe themselves human. Ants around a fat queen (*He laughs.*). . . who is the big-bellied friar. (*ARRIETA questions in sign language.*) They think it's a beautiful day, but I can see the dark clouds. (*ARRIETA points to a section of the painting.*) Yes. The sun is shining in the background. And there is the mountain, but they don't see it. (*ARRIETA signs. GOYA hesitates.*) It's a mountain I know is there.

(*The sounds of the heartbeats have faded and stopped. GOYA jabs his ear and listens in vain. ARRIETA observes him and moves to the left to ask something about the "Two Friars."*)

ARRIETA: (*Pointing*) «What are they doing?»

GOYA: The goat with a beard is deaf too. Who knows what the other one is saying to him? Though perhaps greybeard hears something . . . (*He moves right and turns around.*) Or does he? (*ARRIETA makes a gesture of perplexity. GOYA looks at him enigmatically and turns back to the painting. ARRIETA points to the painting at right, which is behind GOYA'S back, and inquires with brief signs.*) Yes. It's Leocadia. So aware of her splendor. She's in a cemetery.

ARRIETA: «What?» (*We hear a meow. GOYA peers toward the corners of the room.*)

GOYA: The rock where she's reclining is a tomb. (*Another meow. GOYA is silent for a moment and then continues.*) That's where she's put her husband and me. (*He laughs. Several meows coming together distract him.*

ARRIETA *doesn't take his eyes off him. GOYA laughs again.*) The cats are prowling behind the tomb. (*"Two Friars" changes again into "Judith."*)

ARRIETA: «Cats?»

GOYA: They're always around. (*"The Holy Office" changes to "The Pilgrimage." We hear the wing-beats of a gigantic bird. The painter presses one ear and speaks nervously.*) More wine, doctor? (*He goes to the table. ARRIETA shakes his head and cautions him.*) It's pure juice. It won't hurt you.

ARRIETA: «No thank you.»

GOYA: (*As he pours himself a glass*) Do you see "The Pilgrimage"? More insects. They pluck at a lute, scream, and think it's music. They don't know they're in the tomb. (*He drinks. The beating of the wings fades away and stops. GOYA looks into the empty air.*)

ARRIETA: (*His voice perfectly audible*) "Divine Reason!"

GOYA: Exactly. (*He drinks again but is suddenly startled and looks at ARRIETA who is contemplating the painting.*) What did you say? (*ARRIETA, intrigued by his tone, signs.*) Too dark? Is that what you said? (*ARRIETA nods.*) It's that ... they see us dark. They are so luminous ...

ARRIETA: «Who?» (*GOYA watches him as he is thinking. He drains his glass and leaves it on the tray.*)

GOYA. Doctor, I'd like to consult you about something. (*"Leocadia" changes to "The Busybodies." The painter crosses to sit on the sofa.*) Sit here beside me. (*ARRIETA points to the picture and asks about it with signs. GOYA takes time to respond, but he finally does, avoiding eye contact with the doctor.*) Those are two inquisitive women. (*ARRIETA sits beside him. A pause.*) I've been deaf for thirty-one years. At first I heard buzzings, wisps of music. Then nothing. (*ARRIETA nods.*) Nevertheless, since the beginning of the year, the sounds have come back. (*Surprised, ARRIETA questions with his hands.*) Yes, voices too. (*ARRIETA signs.*) Not when I go to sleep, but wide awake. Tiny voices. I know what you're going to say: my mind is creating fantasies to alleviate my loneliness. But I ask you: isn't it possible I've recovered a trace of my hearing? (*ARRIETA shakes his head.*) The voices are ... very real. (*Growing uneasy, ARRIETA shakes his head sadly and traces signs and more signs. Then he gets up, indicating to GOYA that he should not move. He goes to the table and strikes it hard but inaudibly with his fist. He looks at GOYA questioningly.*) No, but ... (*ARRIETA interrupts him with a gesture, picks up the bell, and shakes it with all his might. We hear nothing.*) No! ... (*ARRIETA goes to GOYA'S side and shakes the bell close to his ear. GOYA shakes his head somberly. THE DOCTOR replaces the bell on the table. "The Pilgrimage" changes to "Asmodea."*) So, according to you, it's all in here. (*He points to his* *forehead. ARRIETA nods. Far-off a dog bays.*) If I told you I just heard a dog baying, you'd tell me I didn't. (*ARRIETA shakes his head, confirming it. GOYA gets up and goes upstage.*) Do you find my paintings repulsive? Don't pretend. Everyone does. . . . Maybe I do myself. (*Moved, ARRIETA invites him with a gesture to reject his dark thoughts and points to "Asmodea" with a questioning gesture.*) Asmodea. (*THE DOCTOR'S movements show his surprise.*) Like the crippled devil,* but here it's an angelical she-devil. Below, there are wars, blood, and hatred, as always. It doesn't really matter. They're off to the mountain.

ARRIETA: «To the mountain?»

GOYA: Asmodea carries him off, for he still trembles at what he sees below. He'll still see it from the mountaintop, but the beings that live there will console him. It's a very steep mountain. Flying is the only way to ascend it. (*He laughs. ARRIETA signs.*) Like the sky, but it isn't the sky. (*He decides to show him something.*) Look at this. (*He picks up the painting that is leaning against the wall, brings it downstage, and props it against the table.*) It's almost the same subject. I painted this recently when I finally understood that they aren't flying by magic as I thought . . . (*Points at "Asmodea"*) . . . but with mechanical devices.

ARRIETA: «Who?»

GOYA: (*He looks at him for a moment.*) These bird-men. Their wings are artificial. Below, as you see, the people are burning. The flyers couldn't help them. I don't know why they don't. Perhaps they feel only disgust for us. They must live very happily in those round houses you see above. (*ARRIETA observes it, disturbed.*) I'll show you an etching where you can See them better. I'm not certain the wings are like the ones I've drawn. I used my imagination a little. (*The doctor looks astonished.*) But, of course. You can't see them well from a distance. (*He has said this with a smile. It is uncertain whether he is in earnest or playing a joke on the doctor.*) I won't be long.

(*GOYA exits right. ARRIETA looks at "Asmodea" and the strange smaller painting he has just been shown. LEOCADIA looks in cautiously from left.*)

LEOCADIA: Did you ring the bell?

ARRIETA: Yes. I was trying to prove to him that he wasn't regaining his hearing.

LEOCADIA: What do you think?

ARRIETA: I still don't know.

---

*Reference to the novel *El Diablo Cojuelo* (*The Lame Devil*) by Vélez de Guevara.

LEOCADIA: (*Nervous, she moves closer to him.*) Surely you do! You can see it in his eyes. He's insane. (*Annoyed with her ARRIETA shakes his head without conviction. She goes right to be sure no one is coming and then returns.*) The servants have just told me something dreadful. (*She crosses to peer out from the imaginary balcony.*)

ARRIETA: What is it, señora?

LEOCADIA: Andrés, the coachman, heard it this morning in the market. They're going to announce new decrees. . . . They say they were drawn up by Calomarde and that the king approves them. My God, what will we do?

ARRIETA: For heaven's sake, señora, explain what you're talking about.

LEOCADIA: (*With difficulty*) One decree . . . will pardon anyone who has committed an atrocity on the person or property of a liberal except murderers. (*ARRIETA turns pale.*) They're free to rob, destroy, and attack with impunity.

ARRIETA: And the other decree?

LEOCADIA: The death penalty for all Masons and comuneros, except those who turn themselves in or denounce the rest.

ARRIETA: It may only be rumors. . . .

LEOCADIA: Doesn't it frighten you? Or are you as crazy as he is?

ARRIETA: I'm not crazy and I am afraid. I fear that the government itself may have spread these rumors . . . to provoke attacks.

LEOCADIA: We must escape!

ARRIETA: Don't speak to Don Francisco of these decrees.

LEOCADIA: Not tell him?

ARRIETA: Please, let me think of the best way.

LEOCADIA: And if his life is in danger?

ARRIETA: There's no life without health, señora.

LEOCADIA: There's no health without life!

ARRIETA: Perhaps we exaggerate the danger. Don Francisco has always been respected. . . . (*His words fade away into silence as GOYA'S VOICE is heard offstage and grows louder.*)

GOYA'S VOICE: You're probably wondering, doctor, if all I said about flyers was drivel. (*He enters right, looking at the print he has in his hand.*) Look at this etching. (*He sees them. ARRIETA has stopped talking. Suspicious, GOYA wants an explanation from LEOCADIA.*) Do you want something?

LEOCADIA: (*Shaking her head*) «Nothing.» (*Points*) «I'm going to take away the wine.»

(*She crosses, takes the tray, and exits right under the painter's distrusting gaze.*)

GOYA: That witch has some shady business in store for me today. . . (*ARRIETA has crossed to him and takes the print. Both move to the table, and ARRIETA puts the print down to look at it.*) Look, doctor. This is from a collection I call "Dreams," although they're more than dreams. Do you think it would be possible to fly like that? (*ARRIETA shakes his head.*) Leonardo conceived a similar device. (*ARRIETA begins to sign.*) He didn't fly, but perhaps we will some day. (*He is looking at the doctor mysteriously. ARRIETA returns his stare and shakes his head. LEOCADIA reappears from right and crosses slowly. ARRIETA'S involuntary glance alerts GOYA to her presence.*) You still haven't brought Mariquita!

LEOCADIA: (*We hear her perfectly.*) Mariquita . . . has died. (*She makes a quick exit left.*)

GOYA: Did she say something? (*ARRIETA nods and signs.*) She's going to bring her? (*ARRIETA nods. A silence. GOYA sighs and sits down, brooding behind the table. Finally, he comes to a decision and speaks.*) I'm going to tell you something in confidence, something incredible. Promise me your silence. (*ARRIETA nods, expectant.*) I have seen these flying men. (*He points to the print.*)

ARRIETA: «What?»

GOYA: In the hills beyond. (*ARRIETA slowly takes a seat, observing him with apprehension.*) It must have been two years ago. Far off, but the windows of something that appeared to be a house were shining on the highest point. And they were flying around, very white. (*ARRIETA signs.*) They weren't birds. I thought they might be the French, operating some new machines. But we would have heard about it before now. (*More signs from ARRIETA. GOYA shakes his head and interrupts him.*) No! I'm not dreaming of angels! They live on the earth, but I don't know who they are.

ARRIETA: (*Pointing at Goya's eyes and shaking his head*) «Our eyes can deceive us.»

GOYA: My eyes haven't deceived me. And they've seen our wiser brothers. Maybe they've lived in the mountains for years . . . I'll tell you my greatest desire: that one day . . . they'll come down. To finish off the king and put an end to all the cruelties in the world. Maybe one day they'll descend like a shining army and knock on every door. With blows so thunderous . . . that even I will hear them. (*A silence. ARRIETA observes him and then looks away.*) You think I'm a lunatic. (*ARRIETA shakes his head feebly.*) Let's drop the subject. (*ARRIETA gets up and walks about. He looks first at "The Busybodies" and then at the painter and sadly draws his conclusion. He returns to GOYA'S side and speaks with his hands.*) Of course women still excite me. (*Quick signs from ARRIETA*) Agreed, not as much as before. Painting is more and more important to me and I forget the other. (*ARRIETA signs.*) Troubled? Who isn't? (*More signs*) Now? (*ARRIETA nods. GOYA is thinking how to answer as he sits beside ARRIETA. He takes up the poker and toys with it.*) Now I'm troubled about a letter. (*Gesture of interrogation from ARRIETA*) I wrote to Martín Zapater days ago and I haven't had a reply. I don't think anything's wrong . . . (*Brief pause*) But I was imprudent. Martín is like a brother to me, and I was so in need of getting things off my chest. (*ARRIETA goes through the motions of writing and asks with a gesture.*) Trivial matters. (*He laughs.*) But I did settle accounts with flat nose. (*ARRIETA shows his concern and signs.*) Gross insults? Yes! Fewer than he deserves. (*His smile fades as he sees the expression on ARRIETA'S face.*) You're afraid something has gone wrong? (*ARRIETA signs.*) Two weeks. (*ARRIETA gets up and moves around. We hear the slow, dull sound of a heartbeat.*) I'm not so important to them that they'd open my letters. . . . (*ARRIETA stops and signs. The heartbeats suddenly increase in rhythm and strength.*) I know what the Green Book is. What they say it is. (*ARRIETA signs.*) Thank you. You will write to Martín if it's necessary. But within a few days. Let's hope. (*ARRIETA puts his hand on GOYA'S shoulder and speaks with his other hand.*) To France. (*ARRIETA nods vehemently.*) Do you truly think that . . . I'm in danger? (*ARRIETA nods. GOYA hesitates a moment.*) Of death? (*ARRIETA nods after a moment of hesitation. GOYA stands and begins to pace nervously.*) I must paint here! Here!

ARRIETA: (*Taking him by the arm*) «You must save yourself!»

GOYA: (*Laughing, as the heartbeats grow louder*) I am Goya! And they will respect me!

(*LEOCADIA rushes in from left and goes to his side. While he walks about, she speaks, trying in vain to stop him.*)

LEOCADIA: «They'll drag you in a basket like Riego if you stay! And they'll drag me! And the children!» (*But GOYA shakes his head and goes on speaking, with growing anger above the increasing sound of the heartbeat.*)

GOYA: No, no, and no! Are you listening? We stay here. I'll ask nothing of that big-nosed piece of shit, that murderer! I'll stay with my children, with my painting, and taking my walks through those blessed hills. And I'll celebrate Christmas Eve here, with you, and with your children, and with my family and my grandson.

LEOCADIA: «They'll kill us!»

GOYA: Shut up! Neither you nor the king gives orders here! Here I'm in command!

LEOCADIA: (*Screaming inaudibly*) «Crazy man!»

ARRIETA: (*Coming to her aid*) «Señora, calm yourself and don't upset him. It only makes matters worse.» (*The heartbeats are now very loud. ARRIETA takes GOYA by the arm.*) «Don Francisco, get control of yourself. Come.» (*He leads him to a chair craftily taking his pulse at the same time. GOYA snorts, grimaces, and murmurs some unclear words. The heartbeats gradually fade away. ARRIETA studies GOYA'S face for a few moments; then he takes his hat and cane and signs.*)

GOYA: Accept my apologies, doctor. (*ARRIETA starts left with a goodbye gesture. GOYA'S voice sounds humble.*) Will you come back soon? (*ARRIETA nods, bows, and exits, accompanied by LEOCADIA. The heartbeats are muffled, and their rhythm is like that of a tired heart.*) Child! . . . Mariquita! . . . Where are you? . . . (*He gets up as he speaks and looks out at left. From the right we hear MARIQUITA'S VOICE. He turns around.*)

MARIQUITA'S VOICE: They're leading me through a dark corridor. I can't see.

OLD MAN'S VOICE: "The boogyman's on his way!"

OLD WOMAN'S VOICE: "They've carried her away!" (*Long pause*)

MARIQUITA'S VOICE: You'll never see me again. . . .

(*GOYA has been listening with growing anxiety. The heartbeats, already very faint, cease completely. Silence. The painter mops his forehead with his hand and sighs. The projected paintings are slowly erased, and only the one of "Saturn" reappears. GOYA takes the spyglass and goes to the balcony to look toward the palace. LEOCADIA reappears from left, holding a cup and silently stirring the liquid in it. She looks at him coldly.*)

LEOCADIA: «Drink this.»

GOYA: I don't need a purge.

LEOCADIA: (*Pointing left*) «The doctor ordered it.»

GOYA: (*Shrugging his shoulders*) I won't argue. Let me have it. (*He takes the cup and sits by the table where he leaves the spyglass. As he drinks, LEOCADIA faces him making signs.*) Liberal, yes. But they're not going to hang all the liberals! (*She continues to sign.*) What? (*She signs.*) Old women's gossip!

LEOCADIA: (*Hands together beseeching*) «We must leave!»

GOYA: (*Draining the cup and getting up suddenly*) Do you think I don't see through your game? You're dreaming of France . . . and Frenchmen! (*He seizes her by the arm.*) But you won't put horns on me! I can still make you moan with pleasure or pain. You choose! (*He pushes her away violently, with a look of immense suffering. Fearful but determined, LEOCADIA holds her ground.*) Fetch Mariquita. I haven't seen her all day. (*LEOCADIA looks at him coldly.*) What are you waiting for? (*LEOCADIA signs.*) You've left your children at the house of the architect Pérez?

MARIQUITA'S VOICE: You'll never see me again . . . (*LEOCADIA continues. GOYA is puzzled.*)

GOYA: Safer than here . . . (*Suddenly he understands and takes a step toward her.*) Are you telling me they stay there? (*She nods yes. He is overcome with anger.*) Why? (*She continues.*) Yes, they're your children! But she is my daughter! And she's learning to paint with me, and she's going to be a great painter! I'm the one who decides what's best for my daughter! Her father! (*LEOCADIA shakes her head nervously.*) No, you say? Well, I'll leave now for Tiburcio's house and bring them back. (*She puts herself between him and the door and shakes her head.*) Get out of my way!

LEOCADIA: «Don't bring them back!» (*He tries to leave and she restrains him tearfully.*)

GOYA: Let go!

LEOCADIA: «Wait!» (*She begs him to be calm and signs.*)

GOYA: The child is not afraid. (*LEOCADIA insists with her eyes and makes a circular gesture toward the paintings. The "Saturn" begins to increase in size.*)

LEOCADIA: «The child . . . » (*She indicates her height with her hand.*) «Here . . . » (*Her hands point to the air and to the walls.*) «She's afraid.» (*She mimes the child's fear and crying, pointing to the upstage painting.*) «When she sleeps . . . » (*She mimes the sleeping and waking up screaming and in tears.*)

GOYA: She has nightmares? (*She nods.*) I would have noticed! (*She shakes her head vehemently and points to his ears. Then she takes him by the arm and leads him to the balcony, indicating something to him.*) The Royal volunteers?

LEOCADIA: (*Nodding and forming the word*) «Danger!»

GOYA: (*Without conviction*) They won't bother the children. (*She makes motions to suggest they will, points to the outside, and mimes the action of striking a child, indicating that the volunteers have done it many times.*) Even if it were true, I would have to bring them here for Christmas. (*She shows her perplexity.*) Then I'd have to go to my friend Tiburcio's house every day to see my daughter. (*LEOCADIA shakes her head.*) What do you mean no? (*LEOCADIA points to the balcony again, points to him, and mimes the action of beating. GOYA looks out from the balcony cautiously. The muffled heartbeats resume. LEOCADIA steps back, surveys him with enigmatic eyes, and exits furtively left. The painter shakes his head, turns upstage and, wrapped in thought, contemplates the growing and threatening*) *image of Saturn. Then he collects himself runs left, and shouts.*) Damn witch! What are you plotting now? (*Under the dull heartbeats, he returns to the table, picks up the bell and shakes it. The heartbeats cease. THE PAINTER stops his motions and the beating resumes. Looking at the enormous head of Saturn, he shakes the bell again, and the heartbeats stop. He holds his arm still and they are heard again. The light fades slowly, and when the heartbeats cease, we hear the bell very faintly, followed by faint heartbeats. Then we hear the bell louder and when it stops, the heartbeats are almost inaudible. The bell sounds twice. Silence.*)

Scene 3

The light slowly returns. "Leocadia," "The Holy Office," and "The Reading" are projected on the background. The painting of the flyers has disappeared. LEOCADIA and DONA GUMERSINDA GOICOECHEA are sitting stiffly near the brazier. GUMERSINDA, who is very dressed up, is about thirty-five. Not bad looking and all smiles, her sharp features and keen eyes lack any trace of gentleness.

LEOCADIA: You must pardon the loud ringing. It was the only way he could summon that lout Emiliano.

GUMERSINDA: Please, I understand. How is your master?

LEOCADIA: (*Looking at her sharply, for she understands the intended insult*) Francho? Very happy and well, with the energy of a boy.

GUMERSINDA: For everything, I hope. Does he eat well? How is his cough?

LEOCADIA: It hasn't been long since you saw him. He's the same.

GUMERSINDA: It's just that at his age he could take a turn for the worse at any time.

LEOCADIA: I'm sure he'll be around for a few more years. (*Throwing out a challenge*) I imagine he might even consider marriage.

GUMERSINDA: (*Stunned by her boldness*) God will he doesn't fall into that delusion. Only a strumpet would go along with such a mockery, to inherit his property and put a pair of horns on his head.

LEOCADIA: Don't worry. He isn't considering it yet.

GUMERSINDA: But I still haven't asked you about your dear husband. Is he well?

LEOCADIA: You know I never see him. . .

GUMERSINDA: Forgive me! I'm so forgetful . . . Your husband is still quite young, thank God, and he must be fit and healthy. He's the one with a long life before him. (*She sighs.*) Well, I came to find out, Leocadia, if we would

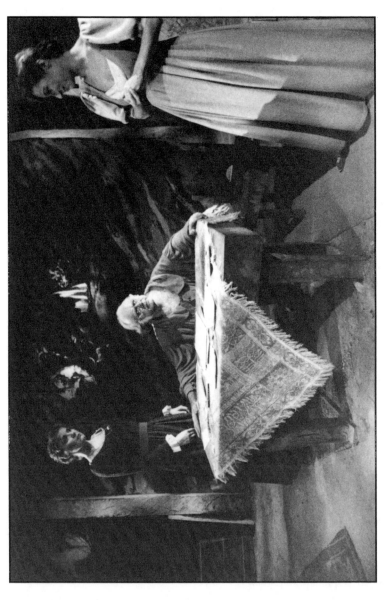

Claudia Hill, Roger Serbagi and Jane Ives in *The Sleep of Reason*. Philadelphia, 1986. Directed by Blanka Zizka. Photo: The Wilma Theatre.

celebrate Christmas here as always. It's the fifteenth of December, and one must make preparations. Will you set up a Nativity Scene this year? Will you let me bring the Three Wise Men to Mariquita?

LEOCADIA: My children won't be here.

GUMERSINDA: No? How is that?

LEOCADIA: (*Hesitating*) Doña Gumersinda, I beg you to help me convince Francho . . . to celebrate Christmas at your house this year.

GUMERSINDA: (*Coldly*) Why?

LEOCADIA: Your father-in-law is in danger. Francho should leave Spain but he refuses to. If he at least left this house . . . and went to yours perhaps . . .

GUMERSINDA: My father-in-law has done nothing wrong. Why do you think he should go into hiding?

LEOCADIA: Others who did nothing have been persecuted and killed.

GUMERSINDA: Our house is not a good hiding place. My husband isn't exactly in favor either . . . as the son of his father. (*She smiles.*) But they're not going to molest either of them.

LEOCADIA: (*Standing, nervous*) And if something does happen to him . . .

GUMERSINDA: I can see that you're afraid, but we shouldn't upset my father-in-law. We'll put on a good face in his presence. (*She steps back and takes a good look at the "Leocadia."*)

LEOCADIA: (*Containing her indignation*) I'll use the little power I have to see that Francho does not spend the holidays here.

GUMERSINDA: Don't think yourself so influential, my dear. And don't call him Francho again. It sounds so ridiculous in your mouth. (*GOYA enters from right.*)

GOYA: (*Warmly*) Gumersinda!

GUMERSINDA: «Father.» (*They embrace. GUMERSINDA gives him a peck on the cheek.*)

GOYA: It's good to see you! Where on earth is my Paco? (*GUMERSINDA shakes her head with a prissy, regretful look.*) What? My heartless son hasn't come with you? (*He laughs.*) But you have brought my grandson to see me? Are you going to tell me where he is? I'll bet he's in the stable admiring the horses. (*He crosses.*) Marianito! Marianito! . . . (*GUMERSINDA runs after him, stops him, and shakes her head.*) What?

GUMERSINDA: «Little Mariano couldn't come . . . »

GOYA: You didn't bring him? (*GUMERSINDA shakes her head, trying to convey humble regret.*)

GUMERSINDA: «Ma-ria-ni-to . . . » (*Placing her hands together in a gesture of asking forgiveness.*) «Asks-you-to-for-give-him. And he sends you kisses.» (*She throws a kiss and then plants a kiss on his cheek.*)

GOYA: Enough. (*He returns the kiss mechanically.*) He didn't come. (*Depressed, he sits down at the table and begins to draw.*)

GUMERSINDA: (*Going over to him and kissing the back of his head*) «Don't be angry with me . . . one of these days I'll bring him. That's a promise . . .» (*She kisses her crossed fingers.*)

GOYA: (*Upset because he doesn't understand her*) Leo! What is she saying? (*LEOCADIA goes to his side and makes rapid signs. GUMERSINDA indicates that it isn't necessary. She takes a pencil and writes on a sheet of paper but LEOCADIA goes on speaking with her hands. GOYA smiles after looking at the paper and at LEOCADIA.*) One of you tells me she'll bring my grandson before Christmas Eve and the other says she won't bring him. Who can trust a woman!

GUMERSINDA: (*To LEOCADIA*) «That's what I said!» (*She points to the paper.*)

LEOCADIA: «I told him what I understood.» (*She uses sign language and GUMERSINDA writes again nervously.*)

GOYA: (*Grimly*) And so it's been for thirty-one years. (*He looks at the paper.*) No, you don't agree. (*To LEOCADIA*) But I can reply to you. I won't hear to celebrating Christmas outside this house.

(*GUMERSINDA smiles, triumphant. Thwarted, LEOCADIA speaks with her hands again. GUMERSINDA caresses the painter; and, touching her temple with a finger she indicates that LEOCADIA is out of her mind.*)

LEOCADIA: «You're evil-minded. You have no shame.»

GUMERSINDA: «Look who's talking about shame.»

LEOCADIA: «You're malicious.»

GUMERSINDA: «Watch what you say.»

LEOCADIA: «It's evil to trick an old man like that.»

GOYA: (*Tired of not understanding, he startles them with a great inaudible blow with his fist on the table.*) The devil can take the two of you! I want you here, seated and quiet. (*He points, and the two women go to the sofa and sit down.*) And now bicker to your hearts' content. But at Christmas, all here, with me. (*LEOCADIA signs timidly.*) Your children too! And no more sour faces! You look like monkeys. (*He becomes absorbed in his drawing. GUMERSINDA and LEOCADIA exchange harsh words in the silence. The exchange between the two women soon becomes bitter again; their gestures show the contempt they feel for each other.*) Didn't the postman come today either? (*They look at him, and LEOCADIA shakes her head.*) Go on. Go on with your sweet chatter. (*He sketches, and they resume their argument. A light cackling sound begins, and GOYA looks up. The cackling grows louder and GOYA *looks toward the sofa, indicating that the cackling appears to come from LEOCADIA'S lips, since she is the one who is speaking at the moment. The sounds increase, it is evident that LEOCADIA is furious. With a haughty gesture, GUMERSINDA interrupts her and replies with a disagreeable bray. GOYA observes them with a strange expression on his face; although he is containing his amusement, there is a trace of terror in his eyes. The cackling sounds and the brays alternate from the mouths of the two women. There is growing surprise in LEOCADIA'S cackles and victory in GUMERSINDA'S brays. Livid, LEOCADIA suddenly stands up and emits two angry cackles which amount to a nervous question. GUMERSINDA rises and responds with a solemn bray that seems a sonorous assertion. Holding his ears, GOYA laughs broadly. They turn to look at him; then at each other. Going over to the old man, GUMERSINDA says goodbye with affectionate kisses.)* You're leaving already? *(She nods and emits a tender little bray. GOYA doesn't know whether to be frightened or to laugh.)* Well, kiss those two ingrates for me. *(GUMERSINDA nods, genuflects, and directs a cold nod of the head to LEOCADIA—which is barely returned—and exits rapidly left. A pause. LEOCADIA is looking at GOYA angrily. Still affected by the joke his ears have played on him, GOYA sketches. We hear a cat's meow. GOYA stops his work and looks somberly straight ahead. LEOCADIA crosses to him, takes his head in her hands and turns it violently so that he can see her. She begins to speak with her hands. GOYA is bothered. A pause. LEOCADIA questions with an imperious movement of her head. GOYA bursts out:)* Gumersinda has a loose tongue!

LEOCADIA: «Then it's true?»

GOYA: *(Throws down his pencil and stands)* Yes! It's true!

LEOCADIA: *(Her movements suggest genuine despair)* «My God! That's how you repay me! That's your love for Mariquita. My children and I will end up begging in the streets!»

GOYA: *(Walking away from her)* What's all the fuss about? . . . Calm down and listen . . . You've got to understand it! *(He takes her by the arm.)* Shut up! *(She screams inaudibly.)* I can't hear you, but shut up! *(She pulls free and sits.)* Pay attention, woman. The king is a monster, and his advisors—jackals he urges on not just to rob but to kill. Protected by the law and the blessings of our prelates! Strip a liberal of his property? He'd better not complain or he'll get the gallows. We're not Spaniards but demons, and they're the angels who are fighting against Hell. I get even. I paint them with the faces of witches and devil worshippers in their rites that they call the Celebration of the Kingdom. But I also get up early, because I'm no fool. Three months ago I went to the notary and ceded this estate to my grandson Marianito. *(LEOCADIA signs excitedly.)* It couldn't be willed to Mariquita!

LEOCADIA: «She's your daughter!»

GOYA: She's my daughter, but not in the eyes of the law or the church! Oh, I don't know why I bother to tell you! (*LEOCADIA moves her hands vigorously.*) I haven't given everything away. I'll put aside special bequests for you . . .

LEOCADIA: (*Stands up and signs as she forms the words with her mouth.*) «They'll take it all. Your son's a greedy opportunist and your daughter-in-law's a witch!»

GOYA: My son is not an opportunist!

LEOCADIA: (*Signing*) «They're waiting for your death like vultures.»

GOYA: They're not vultures! They're not waiting for me to die!

LEOCADIA: (*More signs*) «That's all your good-for-nothing grandson looks forward to!»

GOYA: (*Suddenly wounded, he goes after her.*) Harpy! My grandson is not a good-for-nothing, and he loves me! You're going to respect my Marianito! Do you hear me? (*LEOCADIA is suddenly aware of something at left.*) Do you hear me? (*She motions to him to keep quiet, that something is going on in the house. "Leocadia" and "The Reading" disappear.*) I've had enough of your tricks! You're not going to fool me even if I am deaf. (*She begs him to keep quiet.*) Listen to me, I tell you!

LEOCADIA: (*She whirls around, exasperated, and makes rapid signs.*) «You're impossible! I'm leaving!»

GOYA: Then go! (*He seizes her arm hard.*) Go off with your children and one of those volunteers you flirt with at the bridge.

LEOCADIA: (*Taken aback*) «What?»

GOYA: That fine lad with the moustache! The sergeant!

LEOCADIA: (*Confused*) «What are you saying?»

GOYA: (*He pushes her violently downstage, but she manages an uneasy glance to the left.*) I saw you from here! You can't go off to France to solicit, can you! Whore! (*He shoves her from him and exits angrily right without noticing FATHER DUASO, who has appeared at left a moment before. "The Holy Office" increases in size.*)

LEOCADIA: (*Calling after him*) Francho! . . . Francho! . . .

DUASO: (*Taking off his priest's hat*) You know he can't hear you, señora. (*LEOCADIA turns around in surprise. DON JOSÉ DUASO Y LATRE is a forty-eight-year-old priest. He is unusually tall. His dark hair accentuates the pallor of his delicate and pleasant features. His penetrating eyes reveal his intelligence. Full lips suggest a sensual nature that he combats with constant study and activity. He wears a calotte (skullcap) on the back of his head. The cross of Carlos III gleams on his cassock.*) Forgive me for coming unannounced.

LEOCADIA: I hope Your Reverence will forgive my screaming. Don Francisco . . .

DUASO: (*Raising his hand*) I understand, señora.

LEOCADIA: Please have a seat, Reverend Father. (*She indicates the sofa.*)

DUASO: Thank you. It's better here, if you don't mind. Heat doesn't agree with me. (*He removes his cloak. LEOCADIA hastens to take it and places it on a chair.*)

LEOCADIA: Permit me, Father.

DUASO: Thank you, my daughter.

LEOCADIA: Your Reverence will want to speak with Don Francisco . . .

DUASO: After a chat with you, Doña Leocadia. (*He indicates with a courteous gesture that she should sit on the sofa.*)

LEOCADIA: As Your Reverence commands. (*She sits and DUASO takes the chair behind the table.*)

DUASO: I've been to this house only once before, but I was a neighbor of yours in the Calle Valverde.

LEOCADIA: I remember it very well. Your Reverence is Don José Duaso. (*He gives a little bow with a smile.*) Don Francisco will be very pleased. And I also thank you for your visit, Reverend Father.

DUASO: Why, my daughter?

LEOCADIA: Your Reverence knows to what extremes passions have been unleashed. I fear for Don Francisco.

DUASO: Has anyone bothered you?

LEOCADIA: Not yet.

DUASO: Your concern for him does you honor. If I'm not mistaken, you've served him . . . as housekeeper for some ten years.

LEOCADIA: (*Looking down*) Yes, Father.

DUASO: (*Coldly*) Your husband . . . is he still living?

LEOCADIA: Yes, Father.

DUASO: It's regrettable that you haven't achieved a reconciliation after so long. Incompatibility between husband and wife is, if you will permit me to say so, a great sin.

LEOCADIA: I know, Father, but he disowned me.

DUASO: I'm not unaware of that, my child.

(*A far-off ringing of a bell. LEOCADIA looks left for a moment.*)

LEOCADIA: Someone rang. With your permission, I'll see who it is.

(*She crosses left. DUASO stands up and nods his agreement but continues talking, obliging her to stop.*)

DUASO: I seem to recall that your children live with you. . . .

LEOCADIA: (*Turning around*) So they do, Father.

DUASO: Are they coming of age?

LEOCADIA: My Guillermo is fourteen. (*DUASO approves with a smile.*) And María del Rosario, nine. (*DUASO gives her a hard look. Upset, she adds:*) But she'll soon be ten.

DUASO: Beati pauperes spiritu . . . I shall pray to the Virgin, señora, that those innocent ones will always have good examples and that they'll be raised in the fear of God.

LEOCADIA: (*Embarrassed*) Thank you, Reverend Father.

(*DOCTOR ARRIETA appears at left and bows.*)

ARRIETA: I'm sorry if I've disturbed you.

DUASO: (*Smiles*) On the contrary, Doctor Arrieta. I'm delighted to see you after so many years.

ARRIETA: Very many, Father Duaso. May I congratulate you on your recent honors and advancement.

DUASO: Advancement?

ARRIETA: Did you know, Doña Leocadia? Father Duaso has been named chaplain to His Majesty. And since May he has been in charge of the censorship of publications.

(*LEOCADIA makes a courteous bow of congratulation.*)

DUASO: (*With a grin, after a moment*) I'm from Aragon, my dear Arrieta. And, consequently, very frank. Don't I detect a certain disapproval in your words?

ARRIETA: (*Wary*) I don't understand.

DUASO: Am I wrong to think that you're not pleased with my appointment in the palace nor with my work in the office of censorship?

ARRIETA: I only concern myself with the health of bodies, Reverend.

LEOCADIA: (*Uneasy*) Please be seated. Would you like a cup of chocolate?

ARRIETA: Not for me, Doña Leocadia.

DUASO: Don't bother, señora. And give us the honor of your company. (*LEOCADIA sits. DUASO and ARRIETA imitate her. A sigh from DUASO*) I'm not trying to interrogate you, Doctor Arrieta. I seek only true friendship. People are too silent in Spain, and that's not good.

ARRIETA: True, Father, but a great silence has been imposed, and the censorship Your Reverence exercises proves it. Anyone who dares to break it will pay dearly. But I never took sides in any struggle except the one for our glorious independence. I'm only a doctor.

DUASO: (*Sighing again*) And you only want to speak about the health of bodies. Should I conclude then, seeing you here, that Don Francisco is not well?

ARRIETA: Perhaps.

DUASO: Perhaps?

ARRIETA: Look at the paintings on the walls.

DUASO: Are they his? At first I thought they might be old frescos.

ARRIETA: Because you find them disagreeable, like everyone else.

DUASO: (*Looking at the walls*) They could hardly be considered beautiful. There is so much violence, so much satire in them. Yes, they're his . . . It's a world we've already seen in some of his etchings.

ARRIETA: His etchings were circulated. Now, under the great silence, the painter is consumed, and he cries out from within this tomb so that no one will hear him.

DUASO: Is he afraid?

ARRIETA: Afraid or insane. Perhaps both. And I fear a sad ending . . . Goya is now very old.

LEOCADIA: Father Duaso will not leave us without protection!

DUASO: (*After looking at her to ARRIETA*) Have you thought of a solution?

ARRIETA: For the moment, to get him out of this hole where he must breathe the foul and noxious air of a swamp.

DUASO: From this house, you mean?

ARRIETA: You know I mean this country, Father Duaso. (*DUASO frowns.*)

LEOCADIA: To France!

DUASO: France is the true swamp. . . . Isn't it possible to cure a Spaniard in Spain?

ARRIETA: That is a question Your Reverence must answer for himself. (*A silence. The sound of a flight of giant birds in the air GOYA rushes in from right. They all stand. LEOCADIA runs to his side.*)

LEOCADIA: «What's wrong with you?» (*The painter looks at her wide-eyed. DUASO approaches him.*)

DUASO: «Don Francisco, let me embrace you.»

GOYA: (*Looking at them as if they were all strangers*) It's growing dark. Bring lights, Leocadia. (*She nods and exits left.*) Let them see light in my house; so they'll know it's not abandoned. (*DUASO and ARRIETA exchange perplexed looks. GOYA attempts to regain his composure.*) That I'm at home, with my friends! And with my dogs! Father Duaso, I thank you for your visit. Have they, perhaps, also entrusted you with the censorship of the arts? (*DUASO denies it vigorously.*) If you've come to judge my paintings, don't hide it.

DUASO: (*Opening his arms*) «My son, I come as a friend . . . » (*GOYA looks at him dubiously, but he ends up embracing him with a sad smile.*)

GOYA: Fellow countryman! . . . (*LEOCADIA enters with a lighted lamp and places it on the table.*) Excuse my outburst. No, I'm not crazy; just enraged!

LEOCADIA: «Why?»

GOYA: They've just painted a cross on my door.

LEOCADIA: «What are you saying?» (*They all move quickly to the balcony to have a look. GOYA moves them aside and peers out.*)

GOYA: They've already gone. (*LEOCADIA is distraught. ARRIETA tries to calm her DUASO frowns.*) Have Andrés and Emiliana take a bucket of water and clean the door. (*LEOCADIA exits left.*) Another unclean one: Francisco de Goya. I've heard about those crosses. (*He crosses and turns to face DUASO with a perverse smile.*) Your friends, paisano. (*DUASO shakes his head in denial.*) Forgive me, I don't know what I'm saying. We should all sit down. (*ARRIETA takes a seat near the brazier; DUASO, behind the table.*) And I beside you, so that I can read what you may wish to tell me. (*He hands DUASO a pencil and sits at the end of the table.*) Because it's rained since your last visit . . . (*DUASO is about to write.*) Don't apologize. I'm familiar with your scruples. I'm not a priest, and my housekeeper is a young woman. (*DUASO starts to write.*) And married to boot. (*DUASO lowers his eyes.*) But do tell me how old Goya can be of service to you. (*ARRIETA goes to peer over the balcony. DUASO writes. GOYA reads.*) The way we talk in Aragon, Father. Straightforward. Does your visit have a purpose or not? (*To ARRIETA*) Are they washing away the cross, Doctor? (*ARRIETA nods. DUASO writes. GOYA smiles warmly and presses the priest's hand.*) Thank you. From my heart. I have no need of assistance. (*ARRIETA reacts and sits again. DUASO insists he does and writes again.*) I'm not afraid of that rabble. When they come back, I'll fire on them. (*DUASO shakes his head and writes.*) Don't you believe me? (*DUASO affirms with his head and writes.*) I was never a Mason! (*DUASO writes. LEOCADIA enters left.*) What did those sons of bitches put on the door?

LEOCADIA: «A cross.» (*She sketches it in the air.*)

GOYA: And something more. (*Distressed, she shakes her head.*) I saw them write something, too! What was it? (*She hesitates.*) Answer me! (*She signs. GOYA lets out a mocking grunt and looks at Duaso.*) What they've written concerns you, Father.

DUASO: (*Surprised*) «Me?»

GOYA: They must be theologians. They've written "heretic!" (*DUASO frowns.*) Blessed country, heaven's favorite! Even the criminals work for the Inquisition!
(*Suddenly LEOCADIA runs and throws herself at DUASO'S feet. He stands and tries to lift her up.*)

LEOCADIA: «Please, Father, don't take his words seriously! And save him! Tell him to put aside his pride and accept!»

DUASO: (*At the same time*) «In the name of God, señora, control yourself. You know I've come to be of help! . . .»

GOYA: (*Almost at the same time, he goes to Leocadia's side and manages to get her to her feet.*) For thirty years I've been witnessing a play I don't understand! . . . Get up! . . . (*She stands, gasping silently. DUASO puts his hand on Goya's shoulder and indicates to him to note what he then writes. GOYA remains standing.*) No. I have nothing to ask forgiveness for!

LEOCADIA: «Father Duaso is right! Humble yourself!»

GOYA: I shall not humble myself before the king! (*LEOCADIA steps back in consternation. DUASO writes and GOYA reads.*) What? (*The painter breaks into laughter and begins to walk back and forth. LEOCADIA rushes to the table to read.*) Divine right, you say, paisano? (*DUASO nods.*) Submission to the royal authority even when it's unjust? Church doctrine? (*DUASO looks at him hard without responding.*) What do you think of that, Arrieta? (*Inhibited, ARRIETA points to DUASO.*) Father Duaso, you're no small-time village priest, but a sensible linguist with a chair waiting for you in the Spanish Academy. You don't believe that. (*DUASO confirms that he does energetically.*) You do? And you are certain that the blood of our most beloved Fernando VII is that of his predecessor King Carlos? (*Tightlipped, DUASO writes.*) Well, I do dare to think evil! (*Nervous, DUASO begins to write again.*) Rest assured that our dear Virgin of Pilar did not believe in the virtue of Queen María Luisa. (*Angry, DUASO throws down the pencil and takes a few steps. LEOCADIA makes signs to him to forgive the painter's irreverence and looks at Goya with desperation in her eyes.*) Forgive me, I didn't mean to offend you. (*DUASO looks at him sadly.*)

DUASO: (*His voice is perfectly audible.*) The French infection . . .

GOYA: Yes. You would have said that. Anyone knows what you probably said. (*With a gesture, DUASO declares he doesn't understand. GOYA approaches him in a friendly manner and takes him by the arm.*) Paisano, though I might wish to humble myself before the king, I couldn't. I'd be disobeying him. (*DUASO gives him a look of amazement. ARRIETA stands up.*)

DUASO: «What?»

GOYA: In 1814, when we committed the barbarity of bringing back the "desired one" I did return to the palace. And do you know what he sprung on me? First, that I deserved the gallows. And then, with that tight little smile of his, he ordered me never to appear in his presence until he summoned me himself. (*DUASO looks at him a moment and runs to write, leading GOYA with him. GOYA then reads.*) That is my misfortune. I can't forget that I'm in his hands. But, hidden away in this house . . . perhaps I'll be far from his thoughts. (*Alarmed, LEOCADIA signs.*) Don't offend the priest, woman. A peasant from my land doesn't sell his fellow peasant. So I can tell him frankly how much it saddens me to see him in the service of so bad a cause. (*DUASO writes; GOYA goes on talking.*) When the country was about to revive, they beat and kicked it back into submissiveness. (*DUASO looks at him sharply. "The Holy Office" changes into the "Fight With Clubs." GOYA reads. DUASO writes something and points to what he has written.*) I could have said with clubs. (*DUASO shakes his head and writes. GOYA reads and steps away gloomily.*) Of course I know who Matías Vinuesa was. The priest from Tamajón. An insane fool determined to stain the country with blood. (*DUASO has been writing and shows him the paper GOYA reads reluctantly.*) They were days of danger. They broke into the jail and killed him. (*DUASO writes a single word. GOYA hesitates.*) . . . with blows. (*DUASO shakes his head. A pause. GOYA lowers his voice.*) They beat him to death with their canes. (*A pause. "The Trapped Dog" appears at the left of "Fight."*) But I didn't kill him. I never even followed that horrible fashion of carrying a cane with a little hammer on the hilt. (*DUASO writes.*) Yes, it was a liberal fashion, but . . . (*DUASO writes.*) Yes, I am a liberal. (*The two men look at each other. GOYA goes upstage and contemplates the "Fight." DUASO joins him. GOYA speaks with gravity.*) It's true. We are all participants in crime. (*A pause*) It remains to be known if there are just causes even though crimes go with them. What a trap! Eh, paisano? If you answer that crime erases all justice, then the cause that you serve is not just either. And if you say that there are just causes, we'll go back to arguing which of the causes is the just one. (*Pointing to the painting*) God knows for how many centuries still. (*He turns completely around to face the audience. A pause*) I have painted that barbarism, Father, because I have seen it. And afterwards I painted the lonely dog without a master. . . . You have seen the barbarism, but you stay on at the court, with your master. . . . I am a dog that wants to think and doesn't know how. But, after racking my brain, I reflect on how it was: centuries ago someone took something that was not his. By force. And others responded to that force, and to them still others. . . . And so we've continued. Hammer in hand. (*DUASO moves to the table. LEOCADIA implores him silently. DUASO writes and GOYA continues to speak.*) Don't insist, Father. I won't return to the palace. We'll spend Christmas Eve here, and nothing will happen. With the New Year, we'll decide. First I must finish these paintings! (*DUASO writes and touches his arm. GOYA reads and shows sudden pleasure.*) Will you come by the day before Christmas Eve? (*DUASO nods and smiles.*) And why not spend that blessed night with us? Eh, Leocadia? (*LEOCADIA doesn't conceal her disapproval well after realizing that DUASO is accepting the idea of the painter staying on at the house.*) There'll be candies and sweets, and the local wine is pure honey! And music to the treetops!

DUASO: (*Shaking his head affably*) «I can't.»

GOYA: How sorry I am. No doubt you have your obligations . . . (*DUASO nods.*) . . . at the palace. (*DUASO looks down and ARRIETA watches him.*) Well, until the day before Christmas Eve, Father. I'll show you out. (*THE PRIEST gives GOYA an embrace.*)

DUASO: (*Bowing to ARRIETA*) «God keep you, Doctor.»

ARRIETA: «May he be with Your Reverence.» (*LEOCADIA hands DUASO his belongings. He thanks her with a paternal parting gesture. He extends his hand, and she kisses it. He exits left accompanied by GOYA.*)

GOYA'S VOICE: Bundle up, Father. It's turning cold. (*Sound of glass breaking. A rock wrapped in a paper falls to the floor. LEOCADIA screams. DUASO reappears hurriedly.*)

DUASO: What happened?

ARRIETA: (*Showing him the rock*) Look. (*LEOCADIA attempts to restrain DUASO who tries, angrily, to peer over the balcony.*)

LEOCADIA: Don't let them see you. They may throw another one. (*GOYA reappears left.*)

GOYA: Did you forget something, Father? (*Gradually he understands what has happened.*) A rock?

ARRIETA: «With a paper.» (*He says this while looking at DUASO who approaches and holds out his hand.*)

DUASO: «Give it to me.»

GOYA: (*Coming between them, grimly*) No, paisano! The message is for me. (*He snatches the paper, goes to the table, puts on his glasses and reads.*)

LEOCADIA: «What does it say?»

GOYA: Some artistic advice. They're painters too. (*They look at him perplexed.*) Listen: What is the difference between a Mason and a Mason's lackey? Paint a gallows with an old frog hanging and put underneath: Although I didn't join, I danced to the tune. (*LEOCADIA has to sit down. ARRIETA looks outside.*) Don't show yourself, Doctor. They've probably hidden in the shadows.

LEOCADIA: «Take him away from here, Father Duaso! . . . » (*DUASO starts to write but a gesture from GOYA stops him.*)

GOYA: I won't leave!

DUASO: (*Touching his forehead*) «Are you crazy?»

GOYA: I'm not crazy. And now leave, Father. They won't harm a priest; they're very pious. Nor anyone who goes with him; so you go too, Doctor, with Father Duaso. I'll expect both of you the twenty-third of this month. (*DUASO is about to insist; GOYA cuts him off incisively.*) Go with God! (*DUASO sighs, presses his arm with feeling, and crosses left. ARRIETA bows to GOYA and joins DUASO. Her face revealing her fears, LEOCADIA precedes them, showing the way. The three exit. A pause. Then we hear the far-off baying of a dog, and the painter turns around brusquely to look at the one he has painted. Slow, dull heartbeats become audible. With teeth clenched, GOYA shakes his head; finally, he turns his back on the painting and goes toward the balcony.*) My friends are leaving . . . In the desert again. (*The heartbeats grow stronger. GOYA shakes his head again and with visible effort he tries not to hear anything. The heartbeats fade; the "Fight" changes to "Asmodea," MARIQUITA'S VOICE sounds over the very light heartbeats.*)

MARIQUITA'S VOICE: Others are leaving the house. . . . Now. . . . Don't you hear them?

GOYA: (*He smiles bitterly but he distrusts what he "hears."*) It can't be Leocadia. (*He goes left and then returns, disgusted with himself.*) I won't listen to you. Go. I know you don't exist. (*The heartbeats cease. GOYA looks left, curious in spite of himself.*)

MARIQUITA S VOICE: You don't know. . . (*GOYA stops his ears.*) Stop your ears. . . . How can you block out the voice of your Asmodea?

GOYA: Asmodea?

MARIQUITA'S VOICE: (*In a laughing tone*) My hand gives a soft caress. I'll lead you to the mountain, mountain, tun, tun, tun. . . .

GOYA: (*Trembling*) Mariquita!

MARIQUITA'S VOICE: . . . quita, quita, Mariquita. Mari, Mari, Marasmodea . . . dea, dea, dea . . . Martyr. (*Silence. GOYA grabs his palette and picks up his brushes. When he is about to climb on the ladder LEOCADIA returns, tearful but without outward signs of emotion.*)

GOYA: Tomorrow I'm bringing your children here. (*She shakes her head slowly. She signs. GOYA is silent a moment and then stands motionless, his eyes flashing. Then he puts down his palette and brushes and runs to the door at left.*) Andrés! Emiliana! (*He exits and his voice comes from offstage.*) Worthless trash! Leeches! Is that the way you repay me? I order you to stay! . . . (*Brief pause. GOYA returns.*) They've gone. (*LEOCADIA nods.*) Like rats.

LEOCADIA: (*Her voice perfectly audible*) It's because they aren't crazy. (*GOYA gives her a startled look. Then he looks at "Asmodea" and crosses to the table, poking his ear. He turns around.*)

GOYA: Tomorrow you can go into the city and look for new servants. (*LEOCADIA signs.*) They will come. This is a good house! (*Before she can deny this, she stops short in fear.*) Do you hear something? (*She points toward the balcony. The thumping heartbeats start again. LEOCADIA tries to keep GOYA back from the balcony. He pulls loose and looks out.*) Leo, put out that light. (*She extinguishes the lamp. The paintings fade away; the room remains lighted only by a faint moonglow.)* There are shapes near the door.

LEOCADIA: (*Stifling a scream and pointing outside as she mimics blows on the door.*) «They're beating on the door!» (*The heartbeats are now more rapid.*)

GOYA: Go bar the door! (*He exits left, followed by LEOCADIA. As soon as they disappear the heartbeats stop abruptly and we hear the din of blows, voices, and loud laughter.*)

VOICES: Heretic! Mason! We'll hang you with your bitch! We'll teach you to respect your country. When your tongue's gone, you'll stop your blasphemy, and your whore can speak for you . . .

(Raucous laughter. Blows on the outside door GOYA returns, red with anger and goes to the balcony to peer out. The moment he enters, all the outside sounds cease and the heartbeats, stronger and more rapid, resume. LEOCADIA reappears shortly from left, wringing her hands. Without noticing her the old painter feels the impulse of his Aragonese blood and rushes upstage. He grabs the gun, tests to see if it is loaded and goes right. LEOCADIA screams, shaking her head as she runs to his side.)

LEOCADIA: «No, Francho! Don't do that!»

(GOYA pushes her away and exits right; she follows him. As soon as they leave, the heartbeats stop, and the uproar outside the house is heard again.)

VOICE: (*Along with laughter from the others*) Show yourself, clown, traitor!

LEOCADIA'S VOICE: Francho, for God's sake!

VOICE: Open up, whore! (*Blows on the door*)

LEOCADIA: They'll drag us off, they'll kill us.

VOICE: Open, traitor! We've brought the clubs to break your bones. . . .

LEOCADIA'S VOICE: Give me that gun! . . . (*Moaning*) Give it to me! . . .

VOICE: Are you in bed?

LEOCADIA'S VOICE: (*Sobbing*) Francho, think of me!

VOICE: Cover up, the boogyman's coming! . . .

(Loud laughter which suddenly ceases when GOYA reappears right, followed by LEOCADIA. The heartbeats are heard again, very strong. Bewildered, the painter seems to have lost his daring. Her face covered with tears, LEOCADIA gently takes the gun from his hands and leaves it on the chest. GOYA steps forward and stops dead in front of the table, with a lost look on his face. LEOCADIA crosses and stops in front of the brazier trembling. The two face forward as the heartbeats thunder.)

Curtain

PART TWO
Scene 1

The lights come up on the downstage area. At left THE KING sits embroidering as in the first scene. FATHER DUASO stands waiting respectfully. THE KING looks at him out of the corner of his eye, smiles, and leaves off his needlework.

KING: Well, Father Duaso?

DUASO: Sir, Don Francisco de Goya does not seem inclined to return to the palace. He only aspires to work in the privacy of his country place.

KING: He's a court painter.

DUASO: I suppose, sir, that he feels he's in decline. And since he's not had a commission from the court in years, I believe he prefers not to impose on the palace any paintings that would not be to Your Majesty's taste.

KING: (*Laughs*) You suppose, you believe. There's no doubt of your friendship for Goya. . . . What did he say?

DUASO: (*Hesitating*) I was not able to convince him, sir, that he should ask Your Majesty's indulgence.

KING: (*Sarcastically*) How surprising, Father Duaso. . . . What were his words?

DUASO: (*Embarrassed*) He said . . . not believing he'd done anything wrong . . . he found no reason for seeking your pardon.

KING: (*With a sigh*) Such obstinacy! Liberals never think they've done anything wrong. Did you offer to intercede for him?

DUASO: Yes, Majesty. But he begged me. . . not to make any effort on his behalf.

KING: (*After a moment*) How does he live?

DUASO: Like an inoffensive old man, sir. He decorates his walls with ugly, artless paintings.

KING: Is he afraid?

DUASO: Who can say? He's deaf, and it's difficult to converse with him. He seems tranquil.

KING: Tranquil?

DUASO: Undaunted, at least. But his physician suspects it could be a sign of senility.

KING: Who is his physician?

DUASO: Doctor Arrieta, sir.

KING: Arrieta. . . . His name doesn't sound familiar. Probably some Mason.

DUASO: He appears not to have called attention to himself, sir.

KING: Father Duaso, what can be done? We open our arms lovingly to our children and they reject us.

DUASO: If Your Majesty permits, I'll go back and plead with Goya to prostrate himself before the throne.

KING: (*Nodding*) You may count on my gratitude, Father.

DUASO: I promised Goya to visit him on the twenty-third, the day before Christmas Eve. May I assure him that Your Majesty revokes his former order?

KING: (*Curious*) What former order?

DUASO: Goya has confided in me that, in 1814, Your Majesty told him that he deserved the gallows and ordered him never to appear at the palace until he was summoned.

KING: (*Smiling*) I said that to him in jest! (*He sighs.*) It was a joke. Why would I think that Goya should be hanged?

DUASO: (*Relieved*) Then may I assure him?. . .

KING: (*Cutting him short and smiling*) No. In spite of everything, he's been an opponent of my absolute rights, and he must beg my pardon without my taking the first step. I've given him a discreet nudge through your visit. I only want that hardhead to learn the submission due to the Church and Crown. Do you understand, Father Duaso?

DUASO: I understand and I applaud it, sir. I would like, nevertheless. . . (*He breaks off.*)

KING: (*Affably*) Speak, Father.

DUASO: Majesty, although Goya has asked me not to intercede in his favor, the feelings I profess for him oblige me to do so.

KING: But I've told you, Father, that I'm not going to punish Goya. He only has to beg my pardon.

DUASO: I know, sir. But on the occasion of my first visit I happened to witness an unpleasant incident.

KING: What kind of incident?

DUASO: They painted a cross and wrote the word "heretic" on his door. They threw a stone through the window with an insulting message.

KING: (*Frowning*) Who did this?

DUASO: We didn't see them, sir. It was too dark.

KING: (*Pondering*) We'll have to restrain such excesses.

DUASO: The times are propitious, sir, for other excesses. I fear for my fellow-countryman. If Your Majesty would give me license to be more explicit with him.

KING: Stress the risk he runs, Father Duaso! Perhaps it will persuade him to ask for my favor. Didn't the incident frighten him?

DUASO: Rather it irritated him. (*A silence*)

KING: Fear is also a Christian virtue. (*He lifts the embroidery frame and makes a stitch in the material.*) Did you say you would visit him soon?

DUASO: The twenty-third, sir. (*A silence. THE KING makes another stitch.*)

KING: Father Duaso, I'm confident you'll get him to accept our protection. (*Stitch*) But don't go before eight o'clock in the evening.

DUASO: (*Surprised*) Not before eight?

KING: (*Giving him the familiar smile*) For Goya's sake. Someday I'll explain why I'm making this request. You may take it as an order.

DUASO: (*Perplexed*) I shall, sir.

KING: (*Dismissing him with a movement of his hand*) Thank you for your assistance, Father Duaso. (*He becomes absorbed in his embroidery. DUASO kneels, stands up, and steps back. Blackout.*)

Scene 2

A chorus of faint guffaws. "The Busybodies," "Witches' Sabbath," and "Judith" appear on the upstage wall. GOYA, huddled on the ladder, can be seen in silhouette. Then the lights come up. Wrapped in an old robe to protect himself from the cold, GOYA is working on the figure of the seated woman on the right side of "Witches' Sabbath." From time to time he shivers and blows on his fingers. The brazier table, minus the brazier, shows its mouth. Light, multiple, insistent, the chorus of mysterious laughs peoples the old man's loneliness. He stops to listen, shakes his head, and continues painting.

GOYA: Fantasies. (*Two mocking feminine voices stand out from the merry chorus.*) I won't listen! (*He concentrates on his work. The screeching of owls is added to the laughter. Irritated, GOYA stops.*) I'll will the sounds to stop, and they'll go away. (*He paints, making vague negative motions with his head. The screeching and laughter die down. A louder guffaw provokes a silent rebuff from the painter. The noises fade and cease. GOYA makes sure of the silence and sighs. He blows on his fingers, takes up a brush, and goes back to work.*)

MARIQUITA'S VOICE: No. (*GOYA stops abruptly and listens.*) You can't silence the voices. (*GOYA gives his head a twist. A pause*) Am I the one you're painting? (*GOYA looks with surprise at the figure on which he is working.*) Leocadia says it's she, but it's I. A child who doesn't fear the witches. The greatest witch of all. (*She laughs.*)

GOYA: (*Bowing his head*) It's the deafness.

MARIQUITA'S VOICE: Don't believe it.

GOYA: The deafness.

MARIQUITA'S VOICE: I warn you of things happening that you don't see. . . the departure of the servants.

GOYA: I can guess those things! (*A pause*)

MARIQUITA'S VOICE: What were you looking for before all over the house? In her desk, under her pillow?

GOYA: I won't listen. (*He prepares to paint again.*)

MARIQUITA'S VOICE: They no longer throw rocks. They no longer paint crosses. (*GOYA stops to listen but says nothing. The owls screech again, and the two mocking feminine voices laugh in the midst of the din. GOYA puts down his palette and tries to stop his ears.*) She's late. (*He steps down from the ladder blowing on his fingers, and surveys the road from the balcony. The voice whispers.*) She's always late, for days now . . . (*Tenuous chorus of laughter*) Yesterday you were bent on going to the hills . . . (*A silence*) To look for me.

GOYA: I'm not crazy. I know where my Mariquita is. . . .

MARIQUITA'S VOICE: I'm there. But the thousand-year-old child . . . is in the hills. (*The painter returns to the table and sits gloomily.*) When you came back yesterday you noticed something. Evidence of a visitor. A smell perhaps. (*A silence*) Look for the button. (*GOYA is startled. The voice laughs.*) You haven't looked in the jewel case.

GOYA: It might have fallen off his jacket.

MARIQUITA'S VOICE: A sergeant of the Royal Volunteers lost a button? He was hanging around here this morning, and you noticed the missing button. . . .

GOYA: It probably fell off. . . .

MARIQUITA'S VOICE: He could have given it to her as a present.

GOYA: My mind's playing tricks on me. But one thing I know. Even though I'm speaking to you, you don't exist. Why should I suffer? I won't look for the button.

(*Chorus of tenuous laughter. A woman's voice stands out.*)

WOMAN'S VOICE: Don't look for it, dying man. What's left for you on this earth? Not even us.

SECOND WOMAN'S VOICE: Don't look for the button. Look for the memory of us.

WOMAN'S VOICE: You are alone.

SECOND WOMAN'S VOICE: Follow the example of that poor imbecile in your painting. (*The TWO VOICES laugh.*)

WOMAN'S VOICE: (*Amid laughs*) Admit that you want to . . . (*With his eyes closed and face contracted, GOYA nods "yes" over and over.*)

SECOND WOMAN'S VOICE: Give yourself pleasure, since she has abandoned you.

WOMAN'S VOICE: We won't laugh. (*GOYA gets up, glances wildly at "The Busybodies" and crosses right. When he is about to exit, he hears MARIQUITA'S VOICE.*)

MARIQUITA'S VOICE: You're not old yet, Francho. Will you look for the button or will you lock the door . . . to remember? (*GOYA hesitates.*) If it were in the jewel case, would you believe me?
VOICES OF THE TWO WOMEN: You are alone.

(*GOYA exits. A long pause during which the central painting changes to "The Fates." From offstage left, panting sounds from LEOCADIA who is climbing the stairs with effort. Reaching the landing, she stops to get her breath and enters. Her hair uncombed, she shows the effects of the hard duties required of her since the departure of the servants. She is almost ugly. She is wearing a cloth shawl over her shoulders. She is carrying the lighted brazier and has a broom under her arm. She is a bit surprised not to see Goya. She lets the broom drop to the floor and places the brazier on its table. After arranging it, she takes a look over the balcony. She sighs, steps back, and picks up the broom with a weak groan that betrays her aches and pains. Trembling with cold, she peers through the door at right. Hearing nothing, she begins to sweep the floor. In a few seconds, "The Busybodies" happens to catch her eye; she stops sweeping, uneasy. Then she looks right again. She returns to her work but it is obvious that she is upset by what she thinks the painter may be doing. GOYA returns moments later. He is walking straight, with his hands in the pockets of his dressing gown. There is a gleam in his eyes, and he appears rejuvenated. For a few moments they stand looking at each other.*)

GOYA: (*Harshly*) You were late getting back. (*Wearily, she begins to sign. He interrupts her with a curt gesture.*) I know! You were buying firewood, feeding the horses . . . (*LEOCADIA resumes her work. GOYA advances, looking at her with anger.*) I don't want your bleeding-martyr looks! New servants will come! (*She shakes her head.*) Gumersinda will bring them! (*She stops sweeping and makes a scornful face. He goes to the balcony and rubs his hands together as he searches for words. She notices his tension and is disturbed.*) Hasn't the postman come? (*He turns around to look at her. She makes a negative gesture with her arms. GOYA continues in a mild voice.*) And yesterday afternoon . . . no one came? (*After a moment, she shakes her head. GOYA steps toward her quickly and then stops. Alarmed by the look on his face, she steps back. He looks away, sits down on the sofa, and warms his hands over the brazier. Glancing at him furtively, she resumes her work. GOYA'S voice gives her a jolt.*) Come here. (*She obeys. GOYA has spoken without looking at her and he continues with his eyes fixed on the brazier.*) Are you still afraid? (*She nods. He looks up at her.*) Eh? (*She nods again.*) I'd say you weren't. You don't speak of leaving any more. . . (*LEOCADIA shakes her head wearily, expressing the futility of further discussion, and starts to leave.*) Wait! Why have you lost your fear? (*She doesn't manage an answer.*) Isn't it a singular change? The intrepid Amazon, the coquette who dreams of France, works like a beast and has no time to be afraid. But she doesn't complain . . . (*Brief pause. LEOCADIA sits beside him.*) And there are no more crosses on the door, and no more rocks through the windows. But I haven't made a deal with anyone. (*Very softly*) Have you? (*LEOCADIA looks down. Her breathing has altered noticeably.*) No answer? (*She slips her hand over his on the sofa.*) Is this your answer? (*LEOCADIA lifts GOYA'S hand to her face and places a long kiss on his palm.*) What are you up to? (*She places his hand against her cheek and signs with her free hand. GOYA smiles sarcastically.*) Have you said you love me? (*She nods, caressing and kissing his hand.*) Then answer my question. (*She makes a gesture of desperation and signs.*) And what have I done all these years but shelter you?

LEOCADIA: (*Embracing him*) «Continue sheltering me . . . you must understand.» (*Abruptly her kisses become ardent. She kisses him on the mouth. She slips into his lap. She grabs Goya's hand and moves it over her body, pressing close to him. Pushing her away with all his strength, GOYA stands up. She holds out her arms pleadingly and then lets them fall inert at her side.*) «Save me.»

GOYA: Whore. (*In tears, she shakes her head. GOYA reaches into his pocket and takes out a metal button which he holds up. LEOCADIA stifles a scream. GOYA makes an affirmative gesture and places the button on the table.*) It's better there. Out of its hiding place. The missing button from a pimp's jacket that you put away like some jewel. (*She shakes her head almost imperceptibly. At the same time LEOCADIA'S VOICE is heard in the air. GOYA is momentarily taken aback.*)

LEOCADIA'S VOICE: Take me!

GOYA: A fine fellow, wasn't he! Handsome, tall . . . everything you lacked, and suddenly you had it. A stud to service you and assure the safety of this house. As payment, your body. But you gave it willingly. (*She denies it. We hear her voice again in the air.*)

LEOCADIA'S VOICE: Do whatever you want.

GOYA: Don't deny it. Don't try your love farce on me! I won't forgive you for that. You were offering yourself to a disgusting old man while you were thinking of him. (*She shakes her head convulsively, but at the same time her voice sounds in the air:*)

LEOCADIA'S VOICE: You are a disgusting old man. . . .

GOYA: (*Inflamed by the tricks his mind is playing on him, of which she is unaware.*) You can't get him out of your mind since you rolled about with him yesterday in this very room! (*Denying it with her gestures, she pleads with him on her knees. But her voice comes through the air.*)

LEOCADIA'S VOICE: You're seventy-six years old! (*GOYA turns red and rushes toward her with his hands like claws.*)

GOYA: Filthy bitch! (*He seizes her by the neck. She manages to get away from him and stand up, moving back from him. His features are contracted; he fights back the tears; very softly he murmurs:*) Seventy-six. (*From the opposite side of the brazier LEOCADIA begins timid signs that he refuses to watch. She comes a few steps closer.*) Leave me alone. (*He looks at her with hatred and sadness.*) Go! (*She shakes her head and begins her pathetic pantomime. She points to the outside, to the lover who is attributed to her and to herself; she joins her two index fingers and denies with her head. Then she kisses her fingers as a cross and raises her right hand in a gesture of swearing.*) Spare me your lies. (*She kisses her crossed fingers again and denies vehemently. She runs to the table, picks up metal button and shows it to him. GOYA looks at her fixedly. She points to the floor—the house—and shakes her head. Then she points toward the outside. GOYA'S voice has a terrible resonance.*) You did not find it in the dust of the road. He gave it to you! (*She affirms what he has said energetically.*) Then? (*LEOCADIA sighs, resolved to continue, and she repeats, pointing to the floor, her denial; then pointing to the outside, she sketches the shape of a bridge in the air.*)

LEOCADIA: «The bridge.»

GOYA: He gave it to you on the bridge? (*She nods.*) He was walking with you. (*She nods. GOYA takes the button from her hand and holds it up.*) And you accepted his gift! (*Embarrassed, she traces a few signs. Pause. GOYA puts the button on the table.*) From fear? (*She nods. He grabs her suddenly.*) And why didn't you throw it in the river?

LEOCADIA: «You're hurting me!»

GOYA: (*Releasing her violently*) More lies!

LEOCADIA: (*Shaking her head and pointing outside*) «He. . .» (*She points to herself*) «Me . . .» (*Her hand describes the syllables that come from her mouth.*) «Said . . .» (*Her finger points to the outside and traces a trajectory to the house.*) «He'll come . . .» (*Points to the floor*) «Here . . .» (*Vague gesture*) «One day . . .» (*She points to the table and mimes the action of picking something up.*) . . . to get the button.

GOYA: He'll come one day so that you can return it to him? (*She nods.*) You lie.

LEOCADIA: «I swear it's true.» (*GOYA is uncertain. Exhausted, she starts to sit near the brazier. GOYA'S VOICE sounds in the air.*)

GOYA'S VOICE: "Who would believe it!"

(Brief pause. We hear a soft meowing. GOYA reacts. After a moment of silence, LEOCADIA'S VOICE is heard in the air. It comes in sonorous gusts that almost fade into inaudibility at times.)

LEOCADIA'S VOICE: Don't you believe your Judith? Your Judas?. . . I'll put an end to you. Judith will take her knife, while the cats wail and the bat flutters in the air and drinks your blood and Judas kisses you and Judith kisses you and sinks the blade into you and screams that you tried to strangle her and she had to defend herself. Beware of Judith, beware of the king; the king is the scaffold and Judith is hell. . . . *(GOYA takes her by the hair and turns her head so that he can look into her eyes.)*

GOYA: How to know? *(She looks at him, her teeth clenched. Her voice vibrates in the air and echoes back.)*

LEOCADIA'S VOICE: A fiery shroud envelopes you and turns to ice. I'll ride by laughing on the croup of a horse as you lie in your icy wrappings. . . . *(LEOCADIA hears something as the words echo; she points left.)*

LEOCADIA: «Someone's knocking. . . » *(She touches the painter's arm to draw him from his abstraction.)* «They're knocking.» *(GOYA slowly comes out of his delirium.)*

GOYA: Someone's knocking at the door? *(She nods. He motions to her to wait and crosses to look from the balcony. LEOCADIA stands up, expectant.)* Doctor Arrieta. *(LEOCADIA exits left. GOYA remains at the balcony and withdraws into himself again.)*

MARIQUITA'S VOICE: *(Very lightly)* Buttons are not given as presents in the street but in the bedroom. *(GOYA closes his eyes.)* Search for me. You're not too old for me. Fathers aren't old to their children, and Asmodea is a thousand years old. I'll take you by the hand, my little child, and you'll never come back.

GOYA: *(He mutters somberly.)* I won't come back. *(He turns around slowly. LEOCADIA and ARRIETA enter left.)* Don Eugenio, come in and have a seat. It's a comfort to know that friends remember you. *(ARRIETA makes an affable gesture and signs with his hands as he crosses to the brazier. GOYA is looking at LEOCADIA.)* Yes . . . yesterday I was walking in the hills. *(ARRIETA signs as he sits down.)* There's no reason to worry. They've left us in peace! *(ARRIETA indicates his doubt; he appears tired.)* Leo, bring some wine. Even if the doctor doesn't approve. *(ARRIETA does not protest, and GOYA observes him closely. LEOCADIA exits right. The painter sits near the warmth of the brazier and holds his hands over it.)* Are you ill? You don't look well. *(ARRIETA shakes his head weakly.)* Is something wrong? *(ARRIETA responds with a vague gesture and begins to sign.)* Thank you, I'm fine. *(More signs)* Melancholy. Personal things.

(*ARRIETA signs.*) Also concern for Zapater. I still haven't heard from him. (*Brief pause. The doctor points to him and to his ear and makes circular motions in the air. GOYA is slow to respond.*) A tiny voice . . . from time to time. I pay it no mind. (*A few signs*) In the hills? What about it? (*ARRIETA points to his own eye and describes the movements of the flyers with his hand. LEOCADIA enters with a tray, a jug of wine, and two glasses already filled. The doctor stands up, and LEOCADIA serves the wine.*)

ARRIETA: «Thank you, señora.»

LEOCADIA: (*As she crosses to put the tray on the table*) «I'll leave you with him, doctor. I still must prepare dinner. Will you excuse me?»

ARRIETA: «By all means, señora.»

(*GOYA watches them talking with the irremediable suspicion of the deaf. As she walks by, LEOCADIA picks up the broom and shows it to ARRIETA.*)

LEOCADIA: «I didn't finish sweeping. We can't get servants.» (*ARRIETA bows and LEOCADIA exits left. He sits again. Silence.*)

GOYA: (*He looks at ARRIETA askance and decides to speak.*) I haven't seen the Bird-Men again, if that's what you were asking. (*Assent from ARRIETA*) And you, Don Eugenio, what have you seen? (*A sad shrug of the shoulders from the doctor*) Chains of prisoners, insults from the mob, corpses along the roads. (*ARRIETA looks down.*) Men are beasts. . . . And something else I can't find words to explain. Something I've noted since I lost my hearing and entered the other world. . . . (*ARRIETA is interested but silent.*) Yes. People laugh, move, speak to me. . . . I see them dead. And then I wonder if I'm not the one who's dead. I used to love life. Picnics on the grass, games, songs, girls. Deafness came and I understood that life is death. A manikin dressed as a duchess laughs and sways in silence. She's not human. In my arms she speaks words I don't know and I tell her sweet nothings that I hear only inside my brain. In the war I saw the wounded scream. It was the same. Puppets. Bombs exploded and I only imagined a great laughter. . . . That's why I love people so much; because I could never give myself completely to them nor they to me. I love them because it's impossible for me to love them. I've forgotten my children's voices. I've never heard Leocadia or Mariquita. I'll die imagining them. How can I ever know who they are? (*Lowering his voice*) How can I know who you are? . . . Ghosts. Am I really speaking with someone? I know. Arrieta's ghost is going to tell me I'm deaf. But all that estrangement . . . must mean something more. (*ARRIETA nods.*) Yes? Is it something more? (*ARRIETA nods vigorously.*) What? (*ARRIETA signs. GOYA reflects a moment.*) We're all deaf? (*ARRIETA nods.*) I don't understand you. (*ARRIETA is about to explain further and GOYA stops him.*) Yes. Yes, I do understand. Pity us all! (*There are tears in GOYA'S eyes. ARRIETA places his hand on GOYA'S.*)

Why do we go on living? (*ARRIETA indicates the walls with a circular gesture.*) To paint like that? These walls are oozing fear. (*ARRIETA looks surprised.*) Yes, fear! Art cannot be good if it is born from fear. (*ARRIETA nods his agreement and signs.*) Against fear? . . . (*ARRIETA nods.*) And who triumphs in those paintings—courage or fear? (*Indecision from ARRIETA*) I delighted in painting beautiful forms, and these are filled with maggots. I drank in all the colors of the world, and on these walls darkness is draining away the color. I loved reason and I paint witches. Yes, in "Asmodea" there is a hope, but so fragile. . . . (*He stands and walks about. ARRIETA bows his head. GOYA points upstage.*) Look at "The Fates!" And the devil-worshipper laughing between them. Well, someone is laughing. It's all too horrible for no one to have a good laugh. I'm the puppet one of them is holding. They'll cut the thread, and the devil's priest will laugh at the rag of flesh whose name was Goya. But I foresaw it! There it is! (*ARRIETA signs.*) Why should I leave Spain? I'll not crawl for a villain like him. I'll paint my fear. (*He grabs the glass he had left on the brazier table and drains it.*) Shall we get drunk, Don Eugenio? (*ARRIETA shakes his head sadly. Impulsively, GOYA presses his shoulder.*) Forgive me, I've made you sad.

ARRIETA: (*Shaking his head and signing*) «I have my troubles too.»

GOYA: Drown them in wine! (*He is about to take the doctor's glass but ARRIETA stops him, his expression altered. GOYA goes to the table and pours himself a glass of wine, observing his friend out of the corner of his eye.*) You've seemed troubled ever since you arrived. (*ARRIETA looks at him and then turns his eyes away. GOYA takes a sip of wine.*) You're keeping something from me. (*ARRIETA signs. GOYA, who watches him attentively, suddenly drains his glass and places it angrily on the table.*) You too? (*He goes toward the doctor. ARRIETA nods with a hopeless look in his eyes.*) When did they put the cross on your door? (*ARRIETA signs.*) Why have you come? You should hide. (*Signs*) I'm like an oak! (*Signs*) But you're a doctor. (*He goes up behind him and places his hands on ARRIETA'S shoulders.*) And my friend. (*Brief pause*) A good doctor. A good painter. Crosses on their doors. Poor Spain. (*ARRIETA stands and walks about in gloom.*) Is there no powerful person among your patients to turn to? (*ARRIETA points to his head, indicating that he is giving it thought.*) If you don't find something better, come to this house. (*ARRIETA smiles, points to him, and traces a cross in the air.*) The cross on my door crucifies me, not you! You'd be in less danger living here. You could celebrate Christmas Eve with us. And you could stay on. (*Timidly*) We'd both be less alone. . . . (*ARRIETA motions to him to be quiet and points left.*) Did the bell ring? (*ARRIETA nods. GOYA runs to the balcony.*) The postman! He's finally come! (*We begin to hear the heartbeats, which continue during the scene. ARRIETA turns toward the door. Moments later LEOCADIA appears in the doorway with a letter in her hand. GOYA goes to meet her.)* Give it to me. *(She hands him the letter. He reads the address.)* Martín Zapater's handwriting. *("The Fates" slowly changes into "Witches' Sabbath." With the sealed letter in his hand, GOYA ponders.)* If I didn't open it . . . *(LEOCADIA and the doctor exchange looks of surprise.)* It would be as if I'd never received it.

LEOCADIA: *(After a moment, with a gesture)* «Shall I open it for you?»

GOYA: I could tear it up without reading it. Not from fear but to combat fear. *(He laughs.)* I'm a fool. I'm trapped and I must play the game to the end. *(He goes to the table, puts on his glasses, and reads the letter. Then he looks up. He seems to be deep in thought.)* Don Eugenio, go back to Madrid and seek friends. My offer stands. *(He leaves his glasses on the table, puts the letter in his pocket and slowly walks upstage. As he passes by LEOCADIA, she stops him.)*

LEOCADIA: «What does it say?»

GOYA: The letter? Dear Martín is worried. He hasn't heard from me in more than a month. *(He moves on and takes up his palette and brushes. LEOCADIA does not conceal her terror.)* My letter was intercepted. If there is a Green Book, I must be in it. The despot is thinking of me.

(LEOCADIA bursts into inaudible moans and slumps down on a chair ARRIETA runs to her side to calm her. For a moment, GOYA watches her dramatic reaction from his island of deafness and then starts to paint. The light fades to total darkness; the heartbeats diminish until there is total silence.)

Scene 3

The lights come up on the downstage area. At right, FATHER DUASO and ARRIETA sit looking at each other. The rest of the stage is dark.

DUASO: Tomorrow is Christmas Eve. I promised Goya to visit him today. I'll go after eight. Will you accompany me, Doctor Arrieta?

ARRIETA: *(With a slight bow)* Perhaps it would be better if we talked afterwards, if you have other obligations.

DUASO: *(Smiling)* My time is my own.

ARRIETA: *(Somewhat perplexed)* Then . . . we could talk on the way, if we leave now. It's quite a distance, and it will already be dark at eight.

DUASO: (*After a moment*) We can chat better here. (*ARRIETA raises his eyebrows; he doesn't understand.*) Is something wrong with our friend?

ARRIETA: Father Duaso, I know that I can trust you. . . .

DUASO: You may be sure of that.

ARRIETA: Goya must go into hiding.

DUASO: What's happened?

ARRIETA: A letter he wrote to Martín Zapater has been intercepted. And he criticized the king in it. (*DUASO sits up in surprise.*)

DUASO: How do you know it was intercepted?

ARRIETA: Zapater has not received it.

DUASO: When was it sent?

ARRIETA: Twenty-two days ago.

DUASO: (*Startled*) Twenty-two days? (*He calculates on his fingers.*) You're not mistaken?

ARRIETA: No.

DUASO: (*After a moment of thought*) Goya must beg the king's pardon without delay. I'll go with him myself.

ARRIETA: Father Duaso, no one has ever known the king to forgive an offense. I beg you to persuade Goya to go into hiding this very day. . . .

DUASO: Where could he go?

ARRIETA: (*Hesitating*) I doubt that his son and daughter-in-law would want to take him in.

DUASO: What about his friends?

ARRIETA: Don Francisco has only two friends left.

DUASO: You and I?

ARRIETA: That's right. And I can't offer him asylum because, as you perhaps know, they've painted a cross on my door too.

DUASO: (*Coldly*) I didn't know. Do you think me capable of taking part in those depraved actions?

ARRIETA: I only meant that you might know of it, as you know of other incidents.

DUASO: Then you, too, are in danger?

ARRIETA: (*Shrugging*) Who isn't?

DUASO: And you've come to seek help for . . . Goya?

ARRIETA: You are a friend and fellow countryman of his—not mine.

DUASO: (*He smiles.*) We'll save Goya. I'll protect you. And I trust it will convince you that we aren't as monstrous as the liberals claim.

ARRIETA: Certainly you aren't. I only pray to heaven that you don't become a victim yourself.

DUASO: I don't understand you.

ARRIETA: (*Gravely*) I'm well acquainted with the excesses of fanaticism. We also suffered under the liberal triennium. Today they call the losers Masons; tomorrow they'll say the same of people like you.

DUASO: (*Haughtily*) Who are "they"?

ARRIETA: The most fanatical. They'll turn against you and perhaps against the king himself.

DUASO: What are you saying, my son!

ARRIETA: I foresee it. The king will set up bullfighting schools and close the universities. But perhaps it will be in vain. . . . There is a tremendous tumor growing in our country and we all want to be surgeons. Blood has run and it will run again, but the tumor will remain. I wonder whether physicians will come someday to cure us or whether the bloodletters will go on cutting us up.

DUASO: (*Sighing*) Man is sinful, and neither you nor I can remedy that. So, let us be humble and save Goya.

ARRIETA: You will save him. But my mind won't be at ease.

DUASO: Why not?

ARRIETA: Saving Goya may destroy him. Under the threat of the man he has insulted he walks a line between terror and insanity. And in that strange struggle of his soul, should I, an ordinary man, quicken the terror of a titan so that he will cease to be what he is?

DUASO: For his health's sake, we must.

ARRIETA: And for his life's sake. Because I am a doctor! And, besides, he's no longer a great painter . . . only an old man who puts smudges on the walls.

DUASO: Then . . .

ARRIETA: That's what I want to believe but I'm not sure! What if those nightmares he paints on the walls are great works? And what if his strength is in his madness? Would I want a giant to become a pygmy because I am a pygmy?

DUASO: You'll carry out your duty as I do mine.

ARRIETA: (*Looking at him intensely*) If I were you, Father Duaso, I wouldn't be so calm either.

DUASO: What do you mean?

ARRIETA: l chose to live in shame and therefore I chose silence. I'm going to break that silence, because your honesty is obvious to me . . . and because I'm already marked.

DUASO: (*Without emotion*) Think before you speak, my son.

ARRIETA: Let's suppose, Father Duaso . . . it's only a supposition . . . that His Majesty hesitated to cause a scandal by executing Don Francisco. He's a renowned artist, he wasn't involved in politics.

DUASO: It would demonstrate that the king is not incapable of benevolence.

ARRIETA: Or of showing caution. And let us suppose he stopped short of a sanction with possible repercussions but wanted to take revenge on the painter. (*ARRIETA ignores a reaction of displeasure from DUASO over his choice of words.*) If the proud Goya begged the king's pardon tearfully and retracted like poor Riego, His Majesty would be satisfied for the moment.

DUASO: Doctor Arrieta, I cannot permit you . . .

ARRIETA: (*Cutting him short*) Then I won't go on. (*Pause*)

DUASO: Forgive me. Continue.

ARRIETA: Thank you. Since Goya won't set foot in the palace, it would not be difficult for the king to send someone to suggest it to him. (*DUASO'S expression changes.*) Understand me, Father, a man desirous of helping a friend . . . who, without being aware of it, is collaborating in the royal plan: that the recalcitrant Aragonese becomes the trembling wreck of a man.

DUASO: You contradict yourself.

ARRIETA: No! If Goya accedes, it will prove that he is afraid; if he doesn't, he'll be taught to fear.

DUASO: You're misinterpreting the situation!

ARRIETA: Did you know of the existence of Goya's letter?

DUASO: With God as my witness, no!

ARRIETA: I believe you. Am I equally wrong to think that the king has spoken to you about Goya?

DUASO: (*Wavering*) I'm not going to answer any more questions.

ARRIETA: Allow me a few words more. A rumor has reached me that confirms the goodness of your heart, Father Duaso.

DUASO: What rumor?

ARRIETA: That you are already hiding in this house some of your fellow-countrymen who are in danger.

DUASO: They say that?

ARRIETA: It is the sad gazette of the conquered, whispered among trusted people . . . . I don't want to know if it's true; if Goya comes to your house, it will be. But you are a priest faithful to the throne. It's unbelievable that Father Duaso would shelter anyone, today or tomorrow, without counting beforehand on the royal tolerance. Or am I wrong?

DUASO: (*After a moment*) I beg you, spare me your questions.

ARRIETA: I won't ask again. But I'll tell you my worst suspicion. You promised to visit our friend today. I'll not ask you why it must be after eight and under no circumstances before. (*DUASO looks at him with increasing anxiety.*) But I suspect we will be committing an irreparable error . . . if we don't hasten our visit to Goya and not wait for the stroke of eight. (*DUASO takes out his watch and looks at it nervously.*) But if you must not go before that hour. . . (*Watch still in hand, DUASO stands and looks at ARRIETA;*

terror comes over his face. ARRIETA stands too.) Father Duaso, if you have been a pawn in some game, don't forget that there can be other pawns. (*Very affected and still trying to find a flaw, he reacts abruptly like someone who realizes he has fallen into a trap.*)

DUASO: No one is going to play with me that way. If we hurry, we can reach his house at seven-thirty. Let's take my coach. (*He puts his watch away and, serene again, walks left. ARRIETA accompanies him and the light follows them. DUASO stops before he exits.*) Those paintings on the walls . . . are they really bad?

ARRIETA: I don't believe they're good.

DUASO: Why not?

ARRIETA: He himself gave the answer in one of his etchings . . . "The Sleep of Reason produces monsters!"

DUASO: Always?

ARRIETA: Perhaps not always . . . if reason does not sleep entirely.

DUASO: (*Sighs*) Abyssus abyssum invocat . . . (*He exits followed by ARRIETA: Fadeout.*)

Scene 4

The stage lights come up slowly. The chairs that ARRIETA and DUASO occupied have disappeared. In lamplight, resting on his arms at the far left of the table—and in the same position as in the famous etching—GOYA dozes. A cold lunar light enters through the balcony. Upstage, the "Old Men Eating Gruel" looms enormous. For several moments nothing happens. Then we hear two heavy blows on the door. The sleeping man stirs. With the blows, pale eerie lights invade the room. A third blow sounds, and the strange lights suddenly increase. The light from the lamp becomes a faint greenish glow. Half-illuminated by the light as it grows brighter an unusual shape becomes visible at left. It is a CARNIVAL FIGURE with the mask of a decrepit old man whose ears are great bat wings. Seated on the brazier table with a thick closed book on his knees, he looks impassively at GOYA. There is the sound of huge wings in the air. Under the masked stare, the painter overcomes his drowsiness with effort and turns to look with surprise at the strange presence.

GOYA: Who are you? (*THE FIGURE does not answer. He opens the book and strikes it sharply a few times. Invoked by the action, another CARNIVAL FIGURE appears at right. It flaunts a cat head, and two enormous tits project under its rags. It is carrying an odd wire muzzle with a huge padlock into which a heavy key is inserted. The painter turns his head. At the same time the muffled sounds of small bells and flute-like laughs come from offstage and are repeated from time to time. GOYA puts his hands over his ears.)* Am I hearing?

(THE CAT FIGURE goes up to GOYA and stops. GOYA looks at both apparitions. THE BAT MAN strikes the book lightly and the jangle of the bells grows louder. GOYA looks toward the door. Two other CARNIVAL FIGURES in pig masks rush in, shrieking stridently as they brandish heavy clubs. Rusty bells hang from their belts.)

PIG FIGURES: You don't know me! You don't know who I am! *(Repeating their chant and laughing, they go up to GOYA, lift him up by his armpits, and carry him to centerstage.)*
GOYA: *(Struggling)* Don't touch me!
BAT-MAN: "No man knows another!" *(Another loud blow on the door. THE MASKED FIGURES become silent.)*
GOYA: I only want to live my life.

(THE BAT-MAN orders silence with a prolonged hiss and points to the table. GOYA watches. From behind the table another MASKED FIGURE emerges and sits delicately in the armchair. THE FIGURE is wearing a black cloak with a hood from which the large horns of a bull protrude. The face is a crude skull.)

HORNED FIGURE: *(Raising its hand)* In the name of the priest from Tamajón. *(Laughing, THE PIG FIGURES raise their clubs and position them over Goya's head.)*
BAT-MAN: No. *(He strikes the book.)* See if he has a tail.
GOYA: A tail? *(He tries to get free.)*
BAT-MAN: *(Reading from the book)* Jews and Masons have tails. Our Lord Jesus Christ inflicted this infernal stigma on them as a warning to Christian souls. Proceed.
(THE PIG FIGURES turn GOYA around.)
GOYA: Don't you dare!
(They lift his coattail and inspect.)
BAT-MAN: Does he have a tail?
FIRST PIG FIGURE: A very long one.
SECOND PIG FIGURE: Thick and hairy.
FIRST PIG FIGURE: Very green.
GOYA: You damn pigs!
SECOND PIG FIGURE: And it moves.

GOYA: I'll squash you, bandits. I'll rip you open like worms!. . .
(*THE HORNED FIGURE makes a sign, and as GOYA is speaking THE PIG FIGURES give him half a turn. THE CAT FIGURE goes up and places the wire muzzle over Goya's face, fastening the lock with a noisy turn of the key. Although his lips continue to utter threats and insults behind the grill, the painter's voice is extinguished.*)

BAT-MAN: Does the accused have something to say?

FIRST PIG. Nothing. (*GOYA protests and moves his lips without making a sound.*)

SECOND PIG. The accused confesses to possessing a tail.

BOTH PIGS. He's a Mason and a Jew.

HORNED FIGURE: His Majesty deigns to embroider a flower.

CAT FIGURE: Long live the absolutely absolute king!

PIGS. (*As they whirl GOYA around, they chant.*) Swallow it, dog! Dirty Freemason! You wanted to end the Inquisition! (*Then they oblige GOYA to prostrate himself on his knees and raise their clubs. THE HORNED FIGURE stands and extends its hands solemnly.*)

HORNED FIGURE: Not yet.

BAT-MAN: Release him. (*THE TWO PIG FIGURES release the painter and step back toward the doors on either side. GOYA watches them, expectant.*)

CAT FIGURE: Meow!

BAT-MAN: His Majesty deigns to embroider another flower. (*THE HORNED FIGURE approaches GOYA who collects himself and moves back toward an exit. THE PIG FIGURE that awaits him there raises a club and shakes its bells. GOYA attempts to cross to the other side, and THE HORNED FIGURE charges him like a bull. GOYA avoids the thrust and runs toward the other door. There the other PIG FIGURE awaits him with club and bells. As he steps back, THE HORNED FIGURE charges again and grazes him. For a moment, the two look at each other motionless. THE HORNED FIGURE charges again, and GOYA barely evades him; he charges again and this time he knocks the painter down. THE CAT FIGURE, which has meowed at each charge, now lets out a strident howl, and the delighted PIG FIGURES jangle their bells.*) Enough. (*THE HORNED FIGURE lifts its head and stands rigid.*) You. (*THE PIG FIGURES begin to approach GOYA with clubs half-raised.*)

CAT FIGURE: Death to the rebels!

BAT-MAN: (*Reading from his book and talking through his nose in a bored manner*) Declared a Jew, Mason, liberal, insubordinate, impertinent, incorrigible engraver, painter, masturbator . . .

CAT FIGURE: "What a golden beak!" (*THE PIG FIGURES are near GOYA who is on the floor with his back to them.*)

BAT-MAN: We deliver you to the secular arm.

CAT FIGURE: Long live the spotless king and death to the nation!

PIG FIGURES. (*They lift their clubs slowly and chant a deep accompaniment.*) Swallow it, dog . . . etc.

(*LEOCADIA appears at the left dressed as the Judith of the painting and with a great knife in her hand.*)

LEOCADIA: Quiet, all of you! (*They all look at her. GOYA lifts his head and sits up with visible fear.*) I shall be the secular arm. (*GOYA kneels. She goes to his side and, seizing him by his hair, she obliges him to bare his neck. When she extends the blade to cut off his head, there are fierce blows on the door. LEOCADIA straightens up, fearful. The painter's eyes gleam.*) They've come! (*LEOCADIA exits running at right. THE BAT-MAN slams his book shut and stands. The light fades quickly.*)

BAT-MAN: They? (*GOYA beams with joy as he nods his head. The blows are repeated more urgently. THE PIG FIGURES hurriedly lift the painter and replace him in the chair where he was dozing.*) Who are they? (*A beating of giant wings in the air. THE CAT FIGURE hastens to open the lock and free Goya from the muzzle. The light returns eerily.*)

GOYA: The flyers are knocking on all the doors of Madrid! (*A rain of blows on the door*)

ALL: (*Except GOYA and THE HORNED FIGURE*) No! (*They flee screaming and meowing through both doors. THE HORNED FIGURE lifts the painter's chin with unexpected gentleness. The only light comes from the moon and the lamp.*)

HORNED FIGURE: I'll return. (*He slowly pushes Goya's head until the painter is once again dozing on his folded arms. THE FIGURE slips out stealthily and disappears right. Moments later a tremendous banging is heard. "Saturn," "Witches' Sabbath," and "Judith" appear on the upstage wall. GOYA rouses himself and looks up. The blows cease at that very moment. GOYA stands up, his eyes filled with a wild hope.*)

GOYA: They're knocking so loud that even I can hear them! (*He runs to the balcony but is unable to distinguish anything. In her normal attire, LEOCADIA rushes in from right, horrified. She goes to Goya's side and tugs nervously at his arm. GOYA turns and she can only point to the door. Her throat is paralyzed. Rapid heartbeats begin suddenly and continue during the scene. LEOCADIA flees right, pulling free from the old man as he tries to hold her back.*) What's going on? (*GOYA is crossing left to look when FIVE ROYAL VOLUNTEERS appear in the doorway. Their only weapons are sabers. The chinstraps of their helmets frame their lascivious*

smiles. The first of the group is a goodlooking, strutting SERGEANT with a full moustache. A button is missing from his uniform jacket. The two who follow him have their sabers unsheathed. One of the last pair is carrying a cloth bundle. GOYA runs to the chest to get his gun, but one of the soldiers with a saber is quicker and puts his hand on the gun while the other soldier subdues the painter. THE SERGEANT crosses and leans on the back of the sofa; he signals to the soldier carrying the bundle who tosses it on the sofa and then exits rapidly left with his companion.) Thugs! *(One of the soldiers subduing Goya gives him a slap.)* You'll get what's coming to you! *(In the silence filled with heartbeats THE SOLDIERS laugh broadly without making a sound. THE TWO SOLDIERS drag Goya stumbling downstage. THE SERGEANT takes a gag from his pocket.)* Vermin! Let go! *(THE SERGEANT chokes off his words with the gag, knotting it roughly on Goya's neck. The painter struggles in vain. THE SERGEANT leans back against the table, makes a sign, and THE TWO ASSASSINS throw the old man to the floor. When he gets to his knees and tries to stand, he receives a blow with the flat side of a saber. GOYA emits a ferocious grunt; he tries to get away but a second saber blow destroys his resistance. Then the two sabers fall repeatedly in quick rhythm on his body until he doubles over in pain.)*
MALE VOICE: *(In the air)* "For that you were born!"

(The SECOND PAIR OF VOLUNTEERS return from right bringing LEOCADIA. GOYA is no longer crying out against the gag and bears the blows in silence. LEOCADIA, disheveled and with her breasts exposed, is subjected to taunts and rough caresses. They force her to look and she screams. One of the men tries to kiss her and the SERGEANT reacts.)

SERGEANT. «Keep your hands off that woman, I told you!»

(GOYA is helpless and has fallen to the floor like a limp rag. THE VOLUNTEERS sheath their sabers, laughing and uttering insults. One of them goes to the sofa and unties the bundle, while the other one pulls Goya to his knees and holds up his head so that he can see. THE FIRST VOLUNTEER now approaches with a "sambenito"—the penitent's gown of the Inquisition—which he holds up in front of Goya. Instead of the customary flames painted between the crosses, there are black silhouettes of hammers. They all laugh silently and the air is filled with the shrieks of bats and owls. LEOCADIA moans and makes inaudible pleas. THE SERGEANT and a VOLUNTEER support Goya while another VOLUNTEER puts the gown over the painter's head. Then they lift him under his arms and drag

The Sleep of Reason, Teatr Na Woli, Warsaw, 1977.
Directed by Andrzej Wajda. Photo: K. Gieraltowski.

him to the chair where he had been dozing and seat him. LEOCADIA screams and struggles. The heartbeats and shrieks grow louder.)

MALE VOICE: (*In the air*) "Don't scream, silly fool!"

FEMALE VOICE: (*In the air*) "It's better to sit back and enjoy!"

(GOYA looks at LEOCADIA. THE VOLUNTEER goes to the sofa and returns with a cone-shaped cap, while two others tie the old man's hands and feet.)

MALE VOICE: (*In the air*) "All this and more!"

(While the others stand laughing and mocking, THE VOLUNTEER who brought the penitent's cap takes from inside it a black wooden cross and puts it in the painters bound hands. Then he puts the cap on his head, transforming Goya into one of the penitents he engraved and painted so many times.)

FIRST VOLUNTEER. «We'll crack your ugly skull.»

SECOND VOLUNTEER. «With clubs!»

(Smiling, THE SERGEANT crosses toward the sofa under the leering eyes of the VOLUNTEER who is holding LEOCADIA. The other three sway back and forth chanting in front of GOYA.)

VOLUNTEERS. «Swallow it, dog! Dirty Freemason! You wanted to end the Inquisition!» (*They shout in his face and then dance around in a chorus and repeat their soundless chant. THE VOLUNTEER who was holding Leocadia shoves her to the floor at Goya's feet. She grasps the chair looking at the old man through her tears. THE SERGEANT signals from the sofa and the dancers join the other VOLUNTEER, still chanting snatches of the "Swallow it, dog. . ." The animal sounds die away gradually.)*

SERGEANT: (*Going over to the four VOLUNTEERS and speaking to them privately.*) «Take what you want. The house is yours.»

FIRST VOLUNTEER. (*Smiling*) «I'll try the bedrooms!»

SECOND VOLUNTEER. (*Eagerly*) «Let's look for the food!»

(VOLUNTEERS 1 and 2 exit right, almost on tiptoe; on passing in front of the "Saturn," one of them makes a face of mock terror. VOLUNTEERS 3 and 4 exit left with knowing winks. The animal sounds cease completely at this moment. GOYA looks at THE SERGEANT and at LEOCADIA. She continues watching the frightened painter. The heartbeats become stronger and faster. With his eyes fixed on LEOCADIA, THE SERGEANT calmly removes his helmet and tosses it on the sofa. Then he begins to unfasten his baldric. Suddenly LEOCADIA notices that there are no sounds in the room

and looks up in fright. She does not dare to look behind her for she senses that the sergeant is there. The heartbeats speed up. GOYA'S eyes are fixed on LEOCADIA. Then she turns around slowly and sees the smiling sergeant. He lets his baldric fall to the floor. LEOCADIA stifles a scream and runs upstage. But THE SERGEANT grabs her brutally, kisses her fiercely on the mouth, and drags her to the sofa. She struggles, the sofa is overturned, and the thrashing couple disappear behind it. At the same instant a tempest of sounds is unleashed. Shrieks, brays, crowing, and terrifying howls are added to the continuing heartbeats. The pandemonium goes on a few seconds and then calms down a bit, becoming long waves of laughter punctuated by diverse voices.)

FEMALE VOICE: *(Ironic)* "Two of a kind!"

MALE VOICE: *(Indignant)* "It's forbidden to watch!" *(GOYA averts his eyes and gazes into the emptiness.)*

FEMALE VOICE: "Take advantage of the moment!"

FEMALE VOICES: *(Over the laughter)* "And they are like animals!" "And they are like animals!"

MALE VOICE: "There's no hope now."

FEMALE VOICES: "And they are like animals!"

MALE VOICE: "Why?" *(The shrieks and laughter stop. GOYA looks behind the overturned sofa. The heartbeats stop too. MARIQUITA'S VOICE is heard in the deep silence.)*

MARIQUITA'S VOICE: They're hurting me. *(The old man listens trembling.)* What's happening to me, Don Francho? They've broken my hand. My arm is melting. . . . I can't feel my legs, they're a puddle on the floor.

GOYA'S VOICE: "Truth died!"

MARIQUITA'S VOICE: There's something slimy on my cheek. . . . I can't see. . . . Help me!

GOYA'S VOICE: "Divine Reason, don't spare a one of them!"

MARIQUITA'S VOICE: *(Broken)* I can't . . . speak. My tongue . . . my mouth . . . is pus. *(Silence. With immense sorrow, GOYA looks again at the hidden pair. There is an avalanche of howls, and the heartbeats resume, strong and rapid.)*

GOYA'S VOICE: *(Very sonorous)* "There's no one to help us."

(The uproar reaches its peak; then it slowly dies down: the cries cease, the heartbeats lose their rhythm and stop. GOYA'S head falls over as if he had fainted. Silence reigns again. THE SERGEANT'S boots, which had been sticking out from behind the sofa, disappear. He stands up, his clothes in disarray. While he buttons up, he looks at GOYA, who is motionless. He

recovers his baldric and puts it on; he reaches for his helmet and places it on his head. He goes a few steps closer to the painter and looks at him for a moment with an ironic expression on his face. Then he turns around and grins at the woman lying on the floor. Fingering his empty buttonhole, he crosses in front of GOYA, goes to the table and searches. Smiling, he picks up the metal button. He holds it up so that GOYA can see and then puts it away arrogantly. His expression becomes serious; he checks the time on the table clock and walks upstage with a military gait, clapping his hands and shouting inaudibly.)

SERGEANT: «Pascual, Basilio! Get a move on you! It's time to go!» (*He claps again.*) «Hurry!» (*Moments later two of the VOLUNTEERS appear. One of them is carrying a small wooden box in one hand. He is taking bites from a large cake he has in his other hand. THE SECOND VOLUNTEER is holding a ham and is eating something. THE SERGEANT opens the box and approves with a quick gesture. He goes back to GOYA'S side. The painter can hardly open his glassy eyes. THE SERGEANT lifts GOYA'S head and indicates with his free hand for him to wait as he says:*) «We'll be back!» (*Then he exits left, followed by the two VOLUNTEERS who nudge each other and point at LEOCADIA'S body.*)

(*A long pause, during which "Saturn" and "Judith" slowly fade. LEOCADIA pulls herself up and slowly stands, revealing her loose clothing and battered face. Supporting herself against the sofa, she looks at the figure dressed in the penitent's gown and cap. GOYA stares at her without blinking. The "Witches' Sabbath" grows in size. In tears, LEOCADIA takes a few uncertain steps, but there is something in GOYA'S eyes that stops her. But she goes to him, kneels down, and unties his feet. Then she stands, takes the cross from his hands, and unties the cords that hold his arms. Reacting to the pain in his shoulders, GOYA lifts his arms and unties the gag, spitting the rag from his mouth. When he stands, he is like a huge grotesque puppet. With an angry swipe of his hand, he knocks the cap from his head. He keeps on looking at LEOCADIA. Suddenly he runs upstage, although the beating he has received makes him limp and groan. LEOCADIA runs to his assistance, but he stops and refuses her aid.*)

GOYA: You brought them here. (*She shakes her head weakly.*) For your own shameful pleasure. (*She denies it again. He grabs the gun, cocks it, and puts a trembling hand on the trigger.*)

LEOCADIA: (*Frightened*) «Francho!» (*She steps back in terror and stumbles over the overturned sofa. Filled with pain and anger GOYA moves slowly downstage.*)

GOYA: Don't move! And beg God to forgive you. (*He keeps the gun raised from downstage.*) Are you praying? (*With her back still to him, she nods. He thrusts the gun in her face.*)

LEOCADIA: (*Her voice, sorrowful and serene, is perfectly audible.*) Shoot me. (*Without lowering the gun, GOYA reacts and listens to the voice he thinks he has heard. For the moment he perceives nothing. Her voice rises and falls like gusts of wind.*) I'll go on giving myself to others if you don't kill me. I'm guilty, but I don't know who bears the greater guilt. (*GOYA slowly lowers the gun and continues to stare at LEOCADIA'S neck.*) My poor Francho, I've loved you without knowing you. You lived behind a wall, and still I stayed at your side . . . watching over you, enduring a fear that was not yours. The lonely nights . . . the cold bed. From my bedroom I could hear you moan in your sleep, knowing that you would come to me no more . . . and preferring it that way, for you were only a tired old man. Alone, trying to save my children and this house and you and me from your awful obstinacy. . . (*She begins to turn around slowly as her voice continues clearly. She gives GOYA an anguished look and bows her head.*) I should have gone along with the sergeant, given him promises. . . . We were at his mercy . . . And I don't know if I called him with my desire. . . . Shoot me. (*A pause*) What else do you want? Your suspicions torment you. . . . (*GOYA listens with a stunned expression. A VOICE is heard in the air and he looks up.*)

MALE VOICE: "There is no one to help us!"

LEOCADIA: I won't lie to you. . . . He was brutal and he hurt me. Yet I was like a bitch in heat. I was eager . . . under your very eyes. I was thinking with horror . . . and pleasure . . . of our first times together. I used to think of other men when I gave myself to you; now I'll think of you when I give myself to other men. (*With a moan*) Untie my life. Open the only door that's left. (*A silence. He props the gun against the table.*)

GOYA: (*To himself*) I'll never know what you've said. (*He steps forward.*) But perhaps I've understood you at last. (*He stops centerstage and smiles sadly.*) And you've understood me. How funny! A puppet show! Come in, ladies and gentlemen. Laugh at the jealousy of the old Methuselah and the tricks of the cunning young soldier. . . . The old fool threatens his young mistress because he doesn't dare to defy the others. That's the way it was! When they came in, I didn't reach the gun in time because I didn't want to. Because I didn't dare. Pure comedy! (*LEOCADIA breaks into sobs, runs to his side, and throws her arms around him.*)

LEOCADIA: «Francho!» (*A pause*)

MALE VOICE: "There's no one who can break our bond!"

(*GOYA crumples under his sorrow.*)

LEOCADIA: «My poor Francho, they've destroyed you!»

GOYA: Help me. (*Leaning on her he walks to a chair and sits, stifling his moans of pain.*)

LEOCADIA: «Francho, go to bed. I'll take care of you:» (*She tries to remove the penitent's gown, but he objects.*)

GOYA: I'm not hurt. They hit me with the flat of their swords. (*She signs rapidly.*) No, no. There's nothing left to do but rot away as I paint the decay around me. (*She puts her hand on his shoulder and looks at him, frightened by the wild deranged look in his eyes. He murmurs incoherently. LEOCADIA hears something from left.*) "It's the same everywhere, . . . this is how it happened . . . it always happens."

(*Wary and scared, GUMERSINDA appears from left carrying a sack of provisions.*)

GUMERSINDA: «What happened?»

LEOCADIA: «The Royal Volunteers.» (*GUMERSINDA'S hand goes to her mouth.*)

GOYA: Who is it? (*GUMERSINDA leaves the sack on a chair and crosses, not believing what she sees. After making sure that the figure in the penitent's gown is her father-in-law, she reacts with an excessive display of indignation.*) Is it you, Gumersinda? Did you bring the Christmas wreaths? There will be no celebration now. . . .

GUMERSINDA: «Help me get this horrible thing off him!» (*She tries to remove the gown and he resists.*)

GOYA: Leave it be. They don't want me to take it off, and I must obey. (*It is unclear whether he is actually deranged or is making a joke.*) I'll ask Vicente López to give me drawing lessons . . . And you, Gumersinda. . . (*She has moved back a few steps in her amazement. She is convinced he has gone mad and screams.*) Stop screaming! Come here. (*She obeys, managing to control herself.*) I want to ask you to take me to my son and grandson. If I stay here, they'll beat me to death with their clubs. (*GUMERSINDA shakes her head repeatedly and starts screaming again.*)

GUMERSINDA. «You can't go there!»

GOYA: (*Lifting himself up with effort*) Are you denying me asylum?

GUMERSINDA: (*She spreads her arms wide and then joins her hands in supplication.*) «They'll beat us all! You can't come to our house! You must understand! No! No!» (*She screams hysterically.*)

GOYA: (*As she screams*) It's my son's house, and I deeded it to you as I've deeded this place to you! (*His voice has gained strength; he is incensed.*) I'm asking you to save me! And not scream at me! (*Before the unleashed negatives of his daughter-in-law*) Shut up! (*He slaps her. GUMERSINDA swallows hard, and her inaudible screams stop on the spot. Then she frets silently and backs away. GOYA gains control of himself and smiles sadly.*) Once again I've turned my anger on the wrong person. The comedy all over again. Am I no better than those scoundrels? (*Pause.*) What have they turned me into, Leocadia? (*To himself*) What have I done to myself? (*LEOCADIA touches his arm, looking left. Alarmed, GUMERSINDA turns to look too. FATHER DUASO and DOCTOR ARRIETA rush in and with one glance understand what has happened.*)

ARRIETA: «Too late!»

DUASO: «Assist me, doctor.» (*He starts to remove the penitent's gown from Goya.*)

GOYA: No! No!

DUASO: (*Energetically*) «Yes!» (*Between them they remove the gown, which DUASO throws on the floor with scorn. GOYA rubs his sore shoulder.*)

ARRIETA: (*To LEOCADIA*) «Did they beat him?» (*She nods. ARRIETA puts his hand on the painter's forehead and signs rapidly.*)

GOYA: I can still stand . . . even though I'm old. (*With deep melancholy*) Yes. I'm just a feeble old man. An old man at the edge of the grave. (*ARRIETA shakes his head in disagreement.*) A country at the edge of the grave, whose reason sleeps. . . (*The others are perplexed.*) I don't know what I'm saying. Father Duaso, I've lived too long.

MALE VOICE: (*Very softly*) "If it dawns, we will go away."

GOYA: (*Who has heard it*) Look at what they made me wear! They'll come back with their clubs. (*He takes hold of DUASO'S cassock. The priest takes him by the hand, leads him to the table, and then writes.*) You command and I obey. I'll go to your house. (*GUMERSINDA runs to DUASO'S side and kisses his hand as she mouths a confusion of words. DUASO solemnly cuts short her effusion and writes again.*) I give you my permission. When you think it prudent, beg His Majesty, in my name, to forgive me. . . (*DUASO lowers his troubled eyes. GOYA and ARRIETA exchange melancholy looks.*) And to grant his permission for me to go to France to take the waters in Plombières. (*Weighed down by the detested mission he is now concluding, DUASO nods sadly. ARRIETA withdraws somberly to one side.*)

FEMALE VOICE: (*Very softly*) "If it dawns, we will go away !"

GOYA: Leocadia, we'll have to be apart for some time. Will you pack my paintings, my portfolios, and my plates for me . . . . Please carry my things to Father Duaso's house. Then go to the house of Tiburcio Pérez with your children. Tell him that old Goya wishes him a happy Christmas and begs a corner of his home for you. (*LEOCADIA nods. To GUMERSINDA*) Tell my Paco that the animals stay here. That he's to take care of them. (*DUASO*

The final scene of *The Sleep of Reason*,
Gorki Art Theatre, Moscow, 1973.

touches his arm and shakes his head.) No? (*DUASO writes.*) No, Gumersinda. Those monsters have killed the horses and the dogs. The cats probably got away and they'll be meowing tonight when no one's here. . . Father Duaso, if I'm a long time in coming back to this woman, I ask you to watch over her. Don't let them harm her. . . because of me. (*LEOCADIA steps away deeply moved. DUASO and ARRIETA observe her with concern. DUASO nods.*)

MALE VOICE: I know that a man is finishing a piece of embroidery now. . .

GOYA: (*Absorbed*) And he says . . . it has turned out perfectly for me . . . . (*ARRIETA steps forward. GOYA looks at him.*) What did I say?

MALE VOICE: Who causes us to be afraid?

GOYA: The one who is dead from fear himself. A great fear in my stomach. They have conquered me. But he was already conquered.

DUASO: (*Taking him gently by the arm*) «Shall we go?»

GOYA: Yes, yes. Whenever you say. (*They start left.*)

MALE AND FEMALE VOICES: "If it dawns, we will go!" (*Other whispers join the voices; tiny voices of both sexes that repeat, like the swelling and ebbing of the waves.*)

VOICES: "If it dawns, we will go away! If it dawns, we will go!"

GOYA: Will the flyers come? (*The chorus of voices is augmented.*) And if they come, won't they treat us like dogs? (*A little laugh*) The dogs of Asmodea! (*ARRIETA takes him by the other arm.*)

ARRIETA: «Come, Don Francisco.»

(*They take a few steps. GOYA stops, breaks away from his friends and goes to LEOCADIA. The voices are multiplied. GOYA brings his face close to hers. They exchange looks for a moment; hers frightened and expectant, his desperately searching.*)

GOYA: I'll never know.

(*DUASO takes him gently by the arm again. GOYA whirls around and gives his paintings a farewell look. Contemplating them, a strange smile calms his face. Then he leans on his friends and walks left. GUMERSINDA joins the group, humbly mouthing words of comfort. LEOCADIA stands centerstage watching the old painter leave with a sorrowful and mysterious expression.*)

VOICES: "If it dawns, we will go!"

(Repeating and repeating the phrase, the confusion of VOICES advances like a hurricane on the entire theatre, as the stage lights fade and a huge projection of the "Witches' Sabbath" shines through the deafening din.)

Curtain

Goya's *"Black Paintings"*

(In order of first occurrence in the stage directions of *The Sleep of Reason*)

Spanish titles   English translation in play

Part One, Scene 2

1. "Aquelarre"   "Witches' Sabbath"
2. "Saturno"   "Saturn"
3. "Judith"   "Judith"
4. "Asmodea"   "Asmodea" ("Fantastic Vision")
5. "Las fisgonas"   "The Busybodies"
6. "La Leocadia" ("Una manola")   "Leocadia"
7. "El santo oficio"   "The Holy Office"
8. "Dos frailes"   "Two Friars"
9. "La romería"   "The Pilgrimage"

Part One, Scene 3

10. "La lectura"   "The Reading"
11. "Riña a garratazos"   "Fight with Clubs"
12. "El perro"   "The Trapped Dog"

Part Two, Scene 2

13. "Las Parcas"   "The Fates"

Part Two, Scene 4

14. "Viejos comiendo sopas"   "Old Men Eating Gruel"

ABOUT THE TRANSLATOR

Marion Peter Holt is a writer, translator and professor emeritus of Theatre and Spanish at the City University of New York; in fall 1996 he was a visiting lecturer in Dramaturgy and Dramatic Criticism at the Yale School of Drama. His translations of Spanish and Spanish American plays have been staged in New York and London, in Australia, and by regional and university theatres throughout the United States. In 1985, *Choice* named his collection *Antonio Buero-Vallejo: Three Plays* an outstanding university press book of the year, and in 1986 he was elected a corresponding member of Spain's Royal Academy. He is a member of the Dramatists Guild.

TRANSLATOR'S NOTE AND ACKNOWLEDGEMENTS

This translation was completed under a grant from the National Endowment for the Arts. It was first published in a collection of Buero-Vallejo's plays in 1985 by Trinity University Press. It has undergone a few changes and clarifications in the course of several productions, most recently at Chicago's Bailiwick Repertory in 1994. Although the cast list contains seventeen characters plus the offstage voice of Mariquita, the number of actors required can be reduced by doubling, most effectively by using the same performers as the Carnival Figures in the nightmare scene and as the Sergeant and the Volunteers in the succeeding scene. Some productions have eliminated one of the Volunteers. The average playing time is approximately two hours and 40 minutes, including intermission. Different productions will, of course, vary somewhat in length.

To the directors and actors who have brought this translation to life in the United States and England, my gratitude for your daring; to Phyllis Zatlin, Lois Boyd, and the other individuals behind the scenes who have lent support, my thanks; for the financial support that made this edition a reality, my appreciation to the Program of Cultural Cooperation Between Spain's Ministry of Culture and United States Universities. To Martha Halsey, who wears the title "Buerista" with distinction, my appreciation for the personal efforts that have made this new edition of *The Sleep of Reason* possible; to Christopher de Haan a special thank you for the perceptive "A Note on the Play," written for this playscript edition; and for Margaret and Edward Augustine deserved recognition for the careful preparation of camera copy for this complex script.

M.P.H.

CRITICAL REACTION TO THE PLAY

"*The Sleep of Reason* is a great work by an author in his prime, ambitious in the rigor of its political statement and ambitious in its difficult aims for innovation. . . . Buero Vallejo attempts to carry the contact between performance and spectator far beyond the habitual frontier indicated by the proscenium. The dramatist wants the spectator to no longer be an external observer from his seat in the theatre, but Goya himself."

Lorenzo López Sancho
ABC (Madrid)
8 February 1970

"The Wilma Theater has found in *The Sleep of Reason* a play of imagination and insight that proves exceptionally congenial to the company's multimedia sensibility. In addition, the work is a provocative introduction for local audiences to one of Spain's major contemporary playwrights, Antonio Buero-Vallejo."

William B. Collins
The Philadelphia Inquirer
9 October 1986

"In *The Sleep of Reason*, which opened Tuesday night in a visually and aurally fascinating production at Bailiwick Repertory, Goya's world is stunningly realized. . . . The play has been re-envisioned to incorporate the talents of a deaf actor, Peter Cook. And the result is exceptionally powerful."

Hedy Weiss
Chicago Sun-Times
23 March 1994